LOLA
THE ILLUSTRATED HISTORY
1957 TO 1977

www.velocebooks.com

First published in 1997 by Veloce Publishing Limited, Veloce House, Parkway Farm Business Park, Middle Farm Way, Poundbury, Dorchester DT1 3AR, England. Fax 01305 250479 / e-mail info@veloce.co.uk / web www.veloce.co.uk or www.velocebooks.com. ISBN: 978-1-787111-04-2; UPC 6-36847-01104-8. This Classic Reprint edition published February 2017.

Veloce *Classic Reprint* Series

JOHN STARKEY & KEN WELLS

LOLA

THE ILLUSTRATED HISTORY
1957 TO 1977

VELOCE PUBLISHING

THE PUBLISHER OF FINE AUTOMOTIVE BOOKS

INTRODUCTION

For forty years, Lola have been manufacturing racing cars for sale to any customer with the wherewithal to purchase them. Formula One, Two, Three, Can-Am, Indycar, Formula 5000, Formula 3000, Formula Ford ... you name it, and Lola have built a car (or cars) to satisfy the demand of those wanting a well-built, fast and reliable car – always with a chance of winning. Lola hold the record of being the longest lasting manufacturer of racing cars ever – full stop. This takes into account the likes of Ferrari, Lotus, Bugatti and Porsche, all of whom have needed to manufacture road cars in order to survive (a decision that some of them have had cause to regret). Many, many other manufacturers of racing cars have come and gone with the passing of the years, but always Lola have survived, if sometimes only by the skin of their teeth!

Today they work from spacious purpose-built premises in Huntingdon, Cambridgeshire – a far cry from the garage premises in Bromley where it all began, when Lola burst onto the motor racing scene with a little gem of a sports-racing car, the Mark 1.

All this can be attributed to one person: Eric Broadley. He alone is the reason why so many drivers and teams have purchased a Lola. Behind Eric Broadley's quiet exterior is a thoughtful engineer – a man highly skilled in designing fast, sometimes innovative racing cars which would always be user-friendly and came with built-in protection for their drivers in the event of a 'shunt'.

Eric Broadley has been overshadowed in his career by makers of racing cars such as Enzo Ferrari and Colin Chapman, both essentially extrovert people who, of course, are two of the greatest names in motor racing. However, it is arguable that in time Eric Broadley and his company Lola will be seen to be certainly as important, if not more so, than either Lotus or Ferrari.

As these words were written, it was apparent that Lola cars, due to the debacle of the Company's involvement in Formula One in 1997, would need financial re-structuring in order to survive. I hope we can all join in wishing Eric Broadley and his marvellous Company a good future: they have given so much pleasure to so many.

John Starkey

CONTENTS

ACKNOWLEDGEMENTS & PROLOGUE

Ken Wells.

Acknowledgements

First of all my thanks to Norman Wells for letting me have the use of the research into Lola racing cars which his late brother, Ken Wells, carried out before his untimely death. Second, thanks to Guido Romani, David Piper, Jackie Epstein, Autosport, Mauro Borella, Eric Broadley, Clive Robinson, Sid Hoole, Chris Kerrison, Mike Ostroumoff, Laurie Bray, David Hodges and David Cundy for guidance and photographs.

John Starkey

Prologue

The longest lasting and arguably most successful racing car manufacturer of all began in 1957 when two cousins started designing and building racing sportscars which immediately demonstrated a sizeable advantage over the opposition of the day.

Eric Harrison Broadley was born in 1930 and grew up in the bustling town of Bromley in Kent, where his father owned a gentlemen's outfitters business. Eric grew up in an unremarkable atmosphere, surrounded by the cosmopolitan bustle of his father's shop. The Second World War broke out when he was just nine and attending the local high school. Young Eric, like most of the young boys around the area, became very excited about the air battles of 1940 being fought out in the skies above, and he could soon identify any approaching aircraft as friend or foe just by the sound of the engine.

Although he understood his fascination for things mechanical, Eric's father dissuaded him from being an engineer and convinced him to train as a quantity surveyor instead, a job he reckoned would hold far more security for the future. Eric went to night school, having left school at seventeen to take a job in the building trade with a company called 'Treasures'. Studying for his qualifications at night school, he learned much about stress calculations, which would prove useful later on when car building became his career. He also pursued his hobby of building model aeroplanes and boats, and acquired a Myford ML7 lathe with which he built small model engines of 5 and 10cc.

Lola

1

1956-1959

Until Eric Broadley was twenty-five years old his main mechanical interest lay in motorbikes. It was then that his cousin, Graham Broadley, decided to rebuild an Austin Seven he had bought in 1951 and enlisted Eric's help. Graham had been in the Fleet Air Arm and had studied aircraft engine maintenance before going to work as a tailor in Eric's father's shop. Graham insisted that Eric alter/re-design parts of the Austin, and when it was finished he entered Eric to drive it in a 750 club race at Silverstone. History relates that he came in last – but the motor racing bug had bitten!

After rebuilding another Austin Seven, Eric and Graham decided to enter the 1172 class with a special, and they equipped the lock-up garage at the back of the outfitters in the high street and sold the earlier cars. Even so, Eric had to make use of the Myford lathe as well as having to teach himself to weld, and with these skills the new special was swiftly completed. It was typical of the period, with a home-tuned 1172 Ford engine, swing-axle front suspension and a live rear axle, and it was well constructed.

The start of Lola. The 1172 special awaits action at Brands Hatch, 1957.
(Courtesy Lola Archives)

Eric entered many races with the special in 1956, in particular the Colin Chapman Trophy races. The car looked rather like a Lotus 7. To begin with it was not a winner, not until Eric and Graham learned how to tune the 1172 engine for maximum power. Then in 1957, with Eric and Graham's preparation, they started winning. Graham's father did not allow him to race on a Sunday, and consequently Eric did most of the driving.

Somewhere along the way the car acquired the name which was to stick: Lola. Maybe it came from the song – 'Whatever Lola wants, Lola gets', as Eric and Graham were by now devoting a lot of time to their special. Fired by ambition, the cousins sold the 1172 special for £600, and Eric's motorbike also had to go. They saved cash and started building another, more advanced car which would run with an 1100cc Coventry Climax FWA overhead camshaft engine giving 83bhp and independent rear suspension. At this period the 1100cc class was the first rung on the ladder for young drivers who wished to climb to the top in motor racing.

Eric had looked askance at the de Dion rear suspension of the all-conquering Lotus 11, and he drew a suspension which used the driveshaft as the transverse link with the top wishbone made up of a trailing arm. The lower wishbone was built up of three tubes and fitted with eccentric joints in order to adjust camber and toe-in/out. The rear end design also sported a light crown wheel and pinion casing and hub carriers, which were cast in elektron (magnesium alloy) to save weight. At the front was a fabricated double wishbone set-up, utilising Morris Minor uprights. TR2 drum brakes, inboard at the rear with Alfin drums, completed the running gear. An Austin A30 gearbox with Lotus

Eric Broadley. (Author's collection)

close-ratio gears connected the FWA engine to a BMC 4.55:1 differential and T43 Cooper 15-inch wheels were used.

All this was mounted in a strong spaceframe of 20-gauge steel square tubing which was scarf-jointed and bronze-welded. The cousins built the car at the local garage of Rob Rushbrook, a friend who had been to watch them race and had come away impressed. Rob had a machine shop which Eric had asked to use at night in order to save money. The Coventry Climax engine cost them all of £250, and Eric then visited Maurice Gomm's bodyshop (Arch Motors) where he discovered a front end which had been built for Tojeiro but not collected. The front end was modified to fit the new chassis; the rest of the body followed, and in July 1958 the car was finished and registered 600 DKJ. It was unpainted and took a mere six months from the beginning of the project to its completion. The cousins took their new pride and joy to the Crystal Palace race track on 5 July, where Eric drove it in the London Trophy race, using the two heats as a test session.

Two weeks after this Eric was placed second at Snetterton, beaten only by a Lotus 11 driven by Keith Greene, and then the Lola went to Brands Hatch, where it created a mini-sensation, being the first sportscar to lap the track in less than a minute. In the first heat Eric won outright with a margin over the second-placed car of 24 seconds, but in the final he was 'black-flagged' for erratic driving. Eric promptly entered the race for sportscars up to 1500cc and – despite starting from the back of the grid – finished in fourth place.

Three weeks later at the next meeting at Goodwood, Eric hit a bank avoiding a backmarker who spun in front of him. With black eyes and swollen knees he went into work the next day only to receive an ultimatum from his boss at 'Treasures': the job or motor racing. Eric chose motor racing.

With the car entered for the RAC Tourist Trophy at Goodwood on 13 September, and £100 start money offered by Esso, the cousins worked flat out to repair the Lola. Richard, Eric's brother, made a hood so that the car would be eligible for the international regulations under which the race was run.

Despite the gearbox expiring in practice when Eric changed from fourth to first gear, and Rob Rushbrook fitting the carburettors and manifolds only just before the 8.00am scrutineering, the Lola – co-driven with Peter Gammon – finished 16th overall and 7th in class and set fastest lap in class. This was achieved although the crew had to repair a punctured tyre (as there was no spare) and the distributor drive sheared when the finish was within sight.

With the proceeds of the sale of the 1100cc sportscar, to Peter Gammon, and with £1000 capital put up by his father, Eric started Lola Cars Limited by moving into Maurice Gomm's premises at Byfleet in Surrey, where three cars were built. One of the cars was sold to Allan Ross in the USA (who was to become Lola's first US distributor), one to Mike Taylor, and the other was raced by the 'works' for Peter Ashdown. He had driven mainly Lotus Mark 9s and 11s until, in October 1958, he was at a test session at Brands Hatch where he had been trying out an Elva Mark 4. By coincidence Eric was also there with the Lola, and Nick Syrett, the BRSCC secretary, suggested to Eric that he ought to give Ashdown a drive. Despite not liking the idea of another driver in 'his' car, Eric asked Ashdown to try it, and so fast was he that Eric immediately offered him the works drive for 1959.

Easter Monday 1959 saw the three cars lined up for the Chichester Cup event at Goodwood, and Ashdown led a 1-2-3 triumph. The Nürburgring 1000km was next, in June, and Peter Ashdown took a minute off the lap record, but Eric – partnering him – put the car into a ditch when it started to rain, to post a DNF. Peter Ashdown then equalled Jack Brabham's Formula Two lap record at Brands Hatch before winning the two-hour race for 1500cc cars at Clermont-Ferrand. Allan Ross flew over from America to partner Peter Ashdown

Rob Rushbrook. (Author's collection)

for the Tourist Trophy at Goodwood in September, where they finished 6th overall and won their class.

Eric had been commuting to Byfleet from Chelsfield, near Orpington, and now he called Rob Rushbrook to see whether he could use his premises at Bromley, as the commuting was becoming too much. Rob had some land next to his garage and, drawing on Eric's contacts in the building business, the new premises were soon completed. Lola now had several orders for cars to be built owing to the successes of 1959. In 1960 a total of 19 Mark 1s were built at Bromley among the 44 Lola cars of all descriptions built. The three cars made at Byfleet had 'BY' prefix chassis numbers, while the Bromley-built cars had 'BR'. Specialised Mouldings, headed by Jim Clark (no relation to the driver), were based in Upper Norwood, where they now made the bodies in fibreglass.

Charles Voegele of Switzerland brought money to the fledgling company when he ordered a car to be co-driven by Peter Ashdown, and with it the pair

recorded class victories at Sebring and the Nürburgring 1000km. The engine failed at Le Mans – which was hardly surprising as it had not been stripped down after the previous two races! Angus Clydesdale, later to become the Duke of Hamilton, bought BR21 and still owns it today, after a chequered career. Stirling Moss still races BR17, a car owned by Tommy Haydon which, after winning the Leinster Trophy, he sold to South Africa. The new owner promptly placed third at the Rand 9-hours of 1963 (behind David Piper's Ferrari GTO).

Other notable victories by a Mark 1 included those of BR19, which had a Hewland Transaxle and a 1500cc FPF twin cam Coventry Climax engine. Henry Taylor used this car to win a 1961 'clubbie' at Goodwood, defeating 'D' types and Lister Jaguars. One road car, BR13, was built up with thicker bodywork and an FWE 1220cc engine and recorded 54,000 miles before being sold in the early 1980s.

In 1960 the works car of Peter Ashdown won the 1150cc class of the Autosport Sports Car Championship (from BY3 driven by Alan Rees) – a feat Ashdown repeated in 1961. Seven further cars were built in 1961 including BR18, which was bought by Chris Kerrison, who shared the car with Peter Sergent: the pair won their class at the Nürburgring 1000km. Kerrison would go on to drive a Drogo-bodied Ferrari in GT events from 1962-1965 which is still to be seen on the tracks today. Three further cars were built in 1962 as well as a prototype Mark 1A, featuring a Martin-Ford 1500cc pushrod engine.

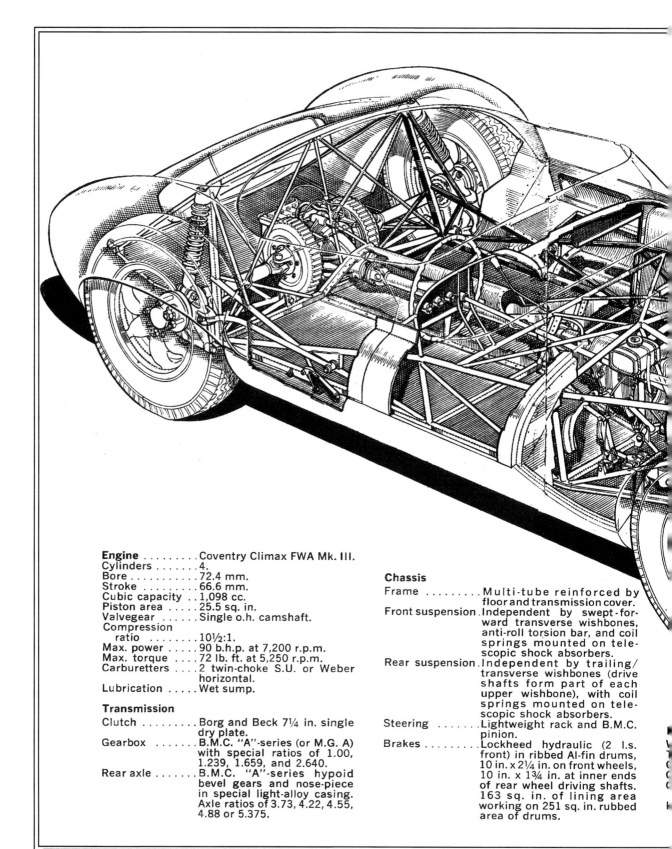

Engine . . . . Coventry Climax FWA Mk. III.
Cylinders . . . . 4.
Bore . . . . 72.4 mm.
Stroke . . . . 66.6 mm.
Cubic capacity . . 1,098 cc.
Piston area . . . . . 25.5 sq. in.
Valvegear . . . . . Single o.h. camshaft.
Compression
  ratio . . . . 10½:1.
Max. power . . . . . 90 b.h.p. at 7,200 r.p.m.
Max. torque . . . . 72 lb. ft. at 5,250 r.p.m.
Carburetters . . . . 2 twin-choke S.U. or Weber horizontal.
Lubrication . . . . . Wet sump.

Transmission

Clutch . . . . Borg and Beck 7¼ in. single dry plate.
Gearbox . . . . . . B.M.C. "A"-series (or M.G. A) with special ratios of 1.00, 1.239, 1.659, and 2.640.
Rear axle . . . . . . B.M.C. "A"-series hypoid bevel gears and nose-piece in special light-alloy casing. Axle ratios of 3.73, 4.22, 4.55, 4.88 or 5.375.

Chassis

Frame . . . . Multi-tube reinforced by floor and transmission cover.
Front suspension. Independent by swept-forward transverse wishbones, anti-roll torsion bar, and coil springs mounted on telescopic shock absorbers.
Rear suspension. Independent by trailing/transverse wishbones (drive shafts form part of each upper wishbone), with coil springs mounted on telescopic shock absorbers.
Steering . . . . Lightweight rack and B.M.C. pinion.
Brakes . . . . Lockheed hydraulic (2 l.s. front) in ribbed Al-fin drums, 10 in. x 2¼ in. on front wheels, 10 in. x 1¾ in. at inner ends of rear wheel driving shafts. 163 sq. in. of lining area working on 251 sq. in. rubbed area of drums.

Lola*

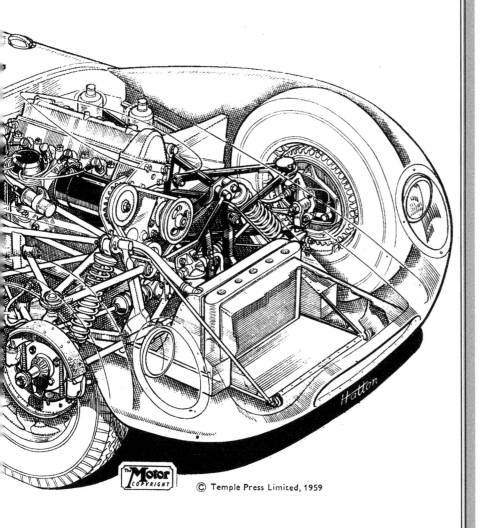

© Temple Press Limited, 1959

In America the Lola had scored well, BR10 being factory fitted with a 750cc OSCA engine to win the 1959, 1960 and 1961 H modified SCCA class driven by Oliver Schmidt, while Allan Ross had sold BY2 to Millard Ripley who went on to win the G Modified SCCA class in 1960. BR23, owned by Charlie Kurz, won its class in the 1961 Sebring 12-hours.

The specials and the Mark 1 Lola had scored an astonishing debut for a small company, and Eric Broadley was about to capitalise on this by moving into single-seat racing car manufacture with his very next car.

nsions

lbase . . . . . 7 ft. 1 in.
. . . . 4 ft. front, 3 ft. 11½ in. rear.
ll length . . . 11 ft.
ll height . . . 1 ft. 11½ in. at scuttle.
d
arance . . . . 5 in.
weight . . . . 7¼-7½ cwt. approx. without
                fuel.

2

1960-1961

Mk 2 – 1960 – FJ/F2/3 – 29 built
Eric Broadley's debut into the world of true open-wheel single-seaters began with the Mark 2 Formula Junior car of 1960. Nicknamed the 'Mini Vanwall' due to its sleek and similar appearance to the World Championship Grand Prix winner, it was the very first single-seater Lola. With a tubular frame and fibreglass body (though the prototype was in

The front suspension of a Mark 2. (Courtesy David Hodges)

aluminium with a Coventry Climax engine) it was front-engined with a Ford 105E on twin SU carburettors. The Mark 2 was notable in several respects, especially in the placing of the engine and transmission. The 997cc Ford and BMC A-series gearbox were offset to the right and canted over at 15 degrees from the vertical. This allowed the propshaft to be offset to the right of the car and it ran alongside the driver's seat, thus allowing a low centre of gravity. The final drive housing was therefore offset by 4.5 inches from the centreline of the Mark 1, and this necessitated unequal-length driveshafts. To counter this Eric Broadley increased the length of the right-hand shaft by placing the outer universal joint inside the hub, thus both driveshafts finished up almost equal in length.

Sean Mooney takes part in the Formula Junior race at Brands Hatch in May 1990 in a Lola Mark 2.
(Courtesy David J Cundy)

The Fitzwilliam team at Monza, 1960. The two Mark 2 Formula Junior cars shown beside the transporter with bodywork removed, were contesting the Trofeo Vigorelli.

The front suspension was the same as that fitted to the Mark 1. The rear suspension featured the aforementioned driveshafts acting as top wishbones, a tubular wishbone operating on taper roller bearings at the hub and a spherical pivot bearing acting upon the chassis. Tubular radius arms completed the suspension which was attached to a spaceframe built up of 20-gauge steel tubes brazed together. A diagonal tube ran from the left front corner of the engine bay to the bulkhead. In consequence, the carburettors had to be detached in order to lift out the engine. After the prototype the rear suspension reverted to that used on the Mark 1. A riveted-on undershield and a stressed propshaft tunnel added to chassis rigidity. An alloy radiator was used to save weight and a six-gallon fuel tank was fitted on the driver's right. Oil for the dry-sump system was supplied from a tank above and to the right of the driver's legs.

Drum brakes (from the Ford Anglia from which the engine had also come) with 'Alfin' finned alloy drums looked after braking; wheels were 13-inch special magnesium alloy castings with front hubs being integral; wheelbase was 82ins; front track was 45ins and rear track was 45½ins Weight was very near the 360kg regulation minimum and the front rear weight distribution was 47/53.

At the Brands Hatch Boxing Day meeting *Autosport* commented on the Formula Junior race, noting the smart new yellow Lola of Peter Ashdown as a definite threat for the future – beaten by only one length by Peter Arundell's well

John Love driving BRJ4, one of the Fitzwilliam team's Mark 2s in 1960.

sorted and more powerful front-engined Elva DKW (powered by a three cylinder/ two stroke Auto Union unit) after an epic race-long dice. Orders poured in and Lola eventually built twenty-nine Mark 2s. Richard Fitzwilliam ordered four cars, one each for John Love, Bill Lacey, Annie Soisbault and Juan-Manuel Bordeau.

These cars had individual coloured nose-cones to tell the pit crews which one was approaching. Love won at Chimay and took third place at Rheims, Albi and the Nürburgring; Dick Prior became Ashdown's co-driver in the 'works' team. Team Speedwell entered Dennis Taylor in a BMC-engined car and Alan Rees and Hugh Dibley also ran Mark 2s.

The Brands race also saw the competition debut of a Cosworth engine installed in the back of the new rear-engined Lotus 18. The Lotus did not work due to a combination of an off-tune engine and the wrong spring settings, but things would change. Jim Clark made his single seater debut there too in a Gemini. All in all, it was quite a historic occasion.

In truth the Lola Mark 2 was unable to keep up with the Lotus 18 Formula Juniors, especially when the Cosworth engine came good and Clark found his knack. Lola did get Cosworth engines, eventually, and the Mark 2 was the best of the front-engined cars. But, good

The radical Mark 3 at the Bromley works. (Courtesy David Hodges)

results, in this transition time from front to rear engine placement, were few and far between.

Michael Bowler track tested a Mark 2 in *Thoroughbred and Classic Cars* November 1977 edition and remarked: 'Sitting in it, you are certainly not obviously conscious of any offset once on the move, and there is no feeling of sitting on the outside of the track; front wheels move up and down nicely ahead of you and you can see the rear wheels in each mirror. The position is pleasantly reclined, if compact, with the right-hand gear lever giving a positive shift to the close-ratio gearbox. The present engine is the Martin Ford rebuilt by Superspeed and is capable of 9000rpm. The car's handling was delightful with the brakes making an excellent job of stopping a mere 9cwt all up; it seemed to handle entirely neutrally, slipping outwards equally at both ends, which bumps didn't seem to upset; you could feel the front moving outwards through the light and sensitive steering. It was a thoroughly nice and viceless car to drive and pretty viceless to maintain too.'

One car was modified and used in F2 by Gerald Smith and Peter Ashdown and known as the Lola Smith. This was probably the Coventry Climax FPF machine which had its transmission running down the left-hand side of the driver and was fitted with 15-inch Lotus 'Wobbly Web' wheels.

It now appears that the Mark 2 prototype had no chassis number and the first production car was listed as BRJ1 (Bromley Junior), etc. Two more Mark 2s later returned to the UK. One is a Formula Two 1500cc with the engine on the 'other' side. The second car is what is reckoned to be the ex-Tony Goodwin Pau GP machine of the early 1960s which had spent some years in the Malaysian jungle sans wheels!

Like most old Lolas, some Mark 2s are still racing. Tony Steele, in particular, has won the Lenham Storage Formula Junior Championship five times in last eight years plus getting second overall and a class win in the 1988 and 1990 FIA Trophies, while Rodney Tolhurst races Peter Ashdown's old car BRJ 13.

At the end of 1960, BRJ15 was raced in the Karlskoga Series and remained in Sweden thereafter, doing clubbie and (possibly) ice racing too! It was purchased in 1965 by Gunnar Elmgren, who was going to have it rebuilt but although work was started by Bill Morris, of ERA fame, it was never completed despite a new Gomm-built body being made in 1970.

BRJ15 was rebuilt for Elmgren by Simon Hadfield, who replaced the 'screamer' with a proper engine. The car uses its original wheels and it has been raced extensively in the last few years including appearances at Monza and also at the Angouleme Street Race in September 1991. *(See Appendix)*

Mk 3 – 1961 – FJ – 11 built

The Mark 2 had not been the success Eric Broadley had hoped for, mainly due to Lola not having access to engines as good as the Cosworth units which were supplied to Lotus for their all-conquering Mark 18, and so Broadley set to and designed his first mid-engined car, the Mark 3, for 1961.

This car featured a fully triangulated frame and was ahead of its time with the driver seated far forward and the fuel tank between him and the engine, just as in modern F1 cars. On top of this, the rear of the spaceframe was quickly detachable by releasing four bolts and the engine connections; a good mechanic needing only twenty minutes to detach the rear end, enabling the engine, gearbox and rear suspension to be worked on in one unit.

Once again the Ford 105E four-cylinder 997cc engine was used, this time tuned by Super Speed Conversions of Ilford, and it featured dry sump lubrication, two twin choke Weber carburettors, different pistons and conrods and modified camshafts. It developed 85bhp at 7200rpm. The engine was canted over at 15 degrees as in the Mark 2, and it drove the rear wheels via a Volkswagen-based final drive/gearbox unit. The Lola-made gears were easily changeable without removing the gearbox, and Eric had commissioned one Mike Hewland to design and build the transaxle, thereby starting off another motor racing dynasty.

Back to the Mark 3's structure. The spaceframe itself was built up of 1 inch and ¾ inch 18-gauge round mild steel tubing. Every bay was triangulated and the undertray, as in the Mark 2, was a stressed member. The front suspension consisted of a twin wishbone set up with an adjustable anti-roll bar, and the coil spring/damper units were mounted outboard. At the rear were the familiar radius arms, two per side, with reversed

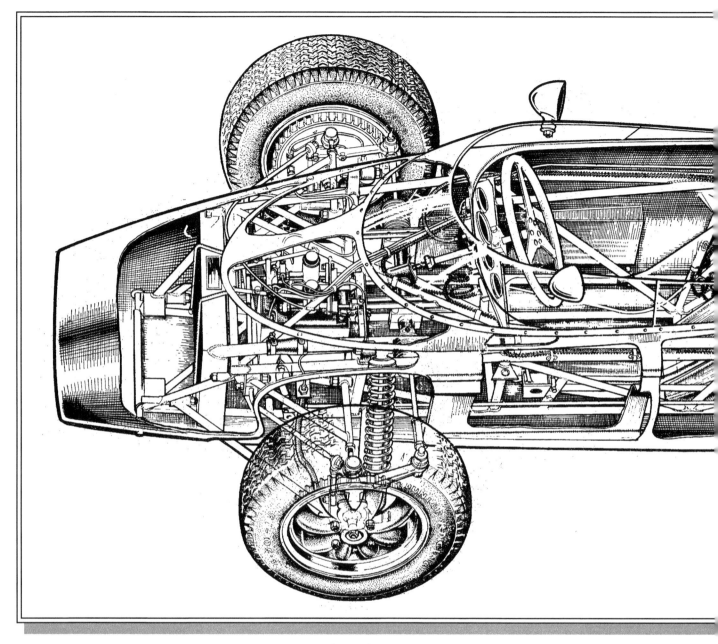

Lola Mark 3.

lower wishbones and the driveshaft acting as the top link; coil spring and damper units came off the back of the rear uprights and connected to the the top rail of the spaceframe. Steering was by rack and pinion mounted on the top frame of the chassis. Triumph Herald uprights were used with specially made steering arms and a front anti-roll bar was fitted. Wheelbase was 88 inches, and front and rear track measured

48 inches. The bodywork was in GRP by Jim Clark's Specialised Mouldings Company.

The Mark 3 was not a success, despite having drivers of the calibre of Peter Ashdown, John Hine, Dick Prior and Dennis Taylor. They, and others such as the Fitzwilliam team, got some good results but were once again hampered by not having the best engines.

Hugh Dibley or Dizzy Addicott drove the Scuderia Light Blue's car, Addicott winning at the Goodwood Members' meeting in July 1961. This car ran in a Formula One race at Brands Hatch in October with a bored-out 1340cc Ford 109E engine. Hugh Dibley drove and came in ninth overall.

Despite such innovation the car was unsuccessful, and as sales died the company almost died too. *Autosport*

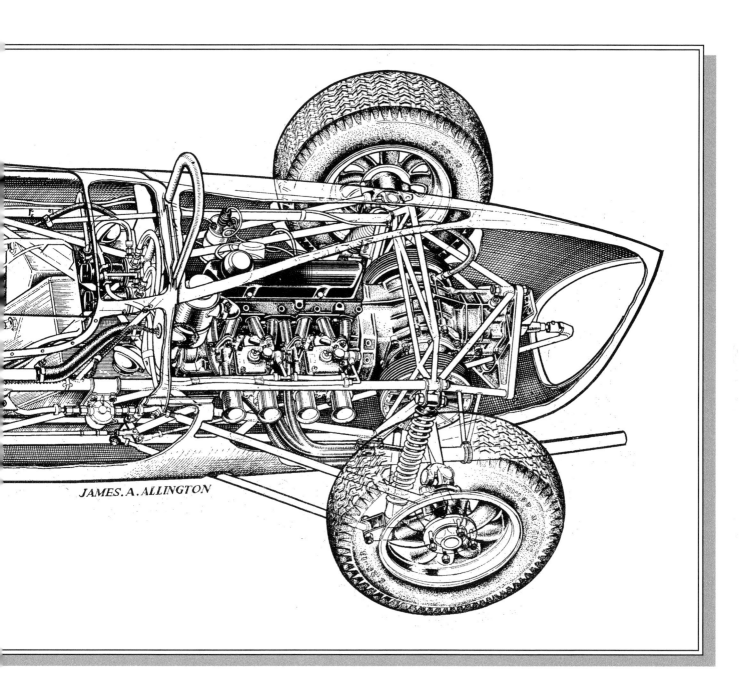

JAMES.A.ALLINGTON

noted in April 1961 that there was no truth in the rumours of a forthcoming Formula One car that year but they were to be confounded by the announcement of Eric Broadley and Lola's next project. (See Appendix)

3

1962-1963

Mk 4/4A – 1962 – F1 – 4 built

For 1962, and just when Eric Broadley thought that financial matters were looking bleak, Reg Parnell, in conjunction with John Surtees, commissioned Lola Cars to build their first Formula One project. Oddly enough, when Surtees had mentioned the project to Colin Chapman of Lotus, that worthy had recommended Eric Broadley! The car was intended for the Yeoman Credit-Bowmaker team whose drivers were Roy Salvadori and John Surtees.

uprights were Standard-Triumph units located by a wide-based lower wishbone and an upper transverse link. At the rear, each wheel hub was fitted into a deep T-shaped casting. A v-shaped upper transverse link gave lateral location and its wide-based (for the time) outboard mounting gave stiffness against toe-in loads. Lateral location was also provided by a lower transverse link while the driveshafts were of the splined variety.

Fairly stiff anti roll bars were fitted front and rear to compensate for the

The Mark 4. John Surtees in the Coventry Climax-engined version at the Nürburgring in 1962 where he finished two and a half seconds behind Graham Hill's winning BRM. (Courtesy David Hodges)

In all, four cars were built using spaceframes with perforated sheet steel bulkheads based on the rear-engined Formula Junior design. Trailing arms from the front and radius rods from the rear suspension took some of the loads through the cockpit. The front

use of relatively low (for the period) roll-centres which were three-and-a-half inches at the front and four inches at the rear. Ten-inch Girling disc brakes were fitted at the front and 9.5-inch ones at the rear. Weight distribution was 45/55 front/rear.

Rear suspension of the Mark 4. (Author's collection)   *Front suspension of the Mark 4. (Author's collection)*

The chassis itself was made up of 1¼ inch, 1 inch and ¾ inch 16, 18 and 20 gauge tubing, and every frame (except for the driver's compartment) was fully triangulated. A removable Y-shaped member was fitted in the top of the engine bay.

The last chassis built had extra sheet aluminium panelling and was known as a 'semi-monocoque'. The engines fitted were first of all the four-cylinder Coventry Climax and then the Coventry Climax V8 with Lucas fuel injection. A Colotti type 32 five speed and reverse transmission was used. A peculiarity of the design was that the chassis tubes doubled as water pipes between the rear-mounted engine and the front-mounted radiator. Fuel capacity was 26 gallons. Chassis numbers began at 41, (Mark 4, number 1).

Surtees recorded impressive times in testing, the fastest ever by a four-cylinder car at Silverstone and Brands Hatch.

In 1962 John Surtees won the Mallory Park 2000 Guineas against good-quality opposition. He also qualified on pole for the marque's World Championship Grand Prix debut at Zandvoort on 20 May 1962, during which the front suspension broke, pitching him into a fence. At Spa 'Big John' found he had difficulty operating the pedals and came into the pits to find his legs pinned together by the fibreglass panel beneath the fuel tank. The engine had run hot, causing the fuel bags to expand and forcing the panel onto Surtees' legs. Loosening the fuel filler cap relieved matters! John Surtees came in second, later in the year, at both Aintree and the Nürburgring.

In all, the Mark 4 amassed 19 points for fourth place in Constructors' Championship standings. Roy Salvadori scored no points in the final World Championship Grand Prix season, not being able to master the Mark 4's

Engine bay of the Mark 4 in the Donington collection. (Author's collection)

Header tank and brake/clutch fluid reservoirs of the Mark 4. (Author's collection)

Dashboard, steering wheel and gearchange of the Mark 4. (Author's collection)

vagaries. Although the car had shown obvious potential, the sponsorship was withdrawn due to poor late-season results, and the team project died. Despite this Lola headed the likes of Ferrari in the Manufacturers' Championship. John Surtees would only take two more years to become World Champion in 1964 with Ferrari.

With the cars converted to four-cylinder 2.7-litre Climaxes for the Tasman series, Surtees won the New Zealand Grand Prix in January 1963. The Mark 4 cars were then raced privately in World Championship events by Parnell and Bob Anderson, the latter winning the non-championship Rome Grand Prix. Chris Amon and Mike Hailwood also raced the Mark 4s and, apparently, John Campbell Jones did too.

Eric Broadley later commented that Lola was a very small company for such a big project, but the F1 cars had shown many more people just how good a designer Eric was ...

As for the surviving Mark 4s, Reg Skeels' article in a 1985 HSCC magazine suggests that one chassis is in the USA (ex-Anderson); the Donington collection has a second, and a third was lost at sea when a boat carrying it sank! Skeels' car is possibly the Surtees/Spa 1962 car by virtue of some identifying structures. It was bought from Tim Parnell (Reg had died) by Reg Hargreaves and Peter Hawtin in the early to mid-1960s for some £800. When they split up Hawtin got the Lola but was killed in a Cooper at a F5000 event at Oulton in 1971. The Lola then went to the Cotswolds and Lincolnshire, acquiring a Buick V8 power unit along the way, until Skeels got it in 1985. Later that same year it was exhibited, engine-less and unrestored, at 'Motor 100'. This car has now been restored to

John Surtees again, this time testing the Mark 4 at Silverstone in 1962. (Courtesy David Hodges)

Chris Amon adjusts his helmet before going out to practice in BRGP44, the Coventry Climax V8-engined car, for the 1963 Italian Grand Prix at Monza.

an exquisite standard by Sid Hoole's establishment.

Mk 5/5A – 1962/3 – FJ – 9 built

Redesigned by Eric Broadley to replace the somewhat disappointing Mark 3, the Mark 5 was alas not particularly successful either. Once again a tubular steel space frame was used, clothed with a glassfibre body. The suspension was by unequal-length links front and rear and anti-roll bars were fitted if required. The driver's seat included the fuel tank and a Cosworth or Holbay engine of 100/105bhp was used. The gearbox was a Hewland Mark 4 and it could be that the Mark 5A suspension was a very early example of push/pull rod, considerably pre-dating modern F1 use.

John Blunsden, writing in a contemporary issue of *Motor Racing*, tested the prototype Mark 5 on the club circuit at Brands Hatch and found the ride reasonably firm without being choppy. Blunsden then went on to praise the exceptional steering 'feel', this despite a rubber joint at the base of the column to iron out extraneous shocks from the track surface; The Lola proved to be a deceptively fast car with only slight understeer and fade-free, powerful brakes. Blunsden said that, in his opinion, if a top-class Junior driver had been in the cockpit, the car would have easily broken the lap record.

In 1962 the Lola Mark 5 was used by the likes of Dick Prior, Dennis Taylor and John Hine. According to some evaluations it was never a true or consistent front-runner, good, but not

Today! Guido Romani driving his Mark 4, BRGP44, during the historic Grand Prix at Monaco in May 1997. This is the ex-John Surtees car of 1962.

that good. However, David Hitches won the Lake Garda race in Italy.

1963 saw the introduction of the Mark 5A, which was an altogether better proposition and one of the fastest

Alan Baillie in the Lola Mark 5. (Courtesy David Cundy)

and most consistent performers in Formula Junior. (This formula, sadly, ceased existence at the end of that year, having brought many drivers, including Richard Attwood, to prominence.) Dickie Attwood was proclaimed the 'most promising new driver of 1963' after winning the Monaco Junior race. David Hobbs and Bill Bradley (later the Lola agent in Germany) were also notable drivers in Mark 5As, as were Andrea de Adamich, Piko Troberg and Eric Offenstadt in Europe. *(See Appendix)*

4

1964-1965

Mk 6 – 1963 – GT – 3 built

1963 was the transition point between the front-engined and the rear-engined racing car. Eric Broadley – in the vanguard of the new designers – saw a gap in the GT class of racing car, and in January 1963 Lola displayed their new contender at the racing car show, to universal acclaim. The Lola Mark 6 coupé was a mid-engined car with a Ford 4.2-litre (256 cu in) V8 engine giving a quoted 350bhp at 7000rpm and driving the rear wheels through a Colotti transaxle. Gear selection was via Bowden type cables instead of the more usual long rod which turned and slid back and forth. Oddly for a racing car, the gear lever was centrally mounted instead of being to the driver's right. The sleek bodywork, designed by John Frayling, was in glass reinforced plastic (GRP) and made, once more, by Specialised Mouldings, the company based in Upper Norwood and headed by Peter Jackson.

The new coupé was based on a monocoque tub which consisted of two D-shaped fuel tanks at each side of the cockpit joined by a stressed skin aluminium floor. In front of this structure was a subframe built up of tubes to support the radiator, and front suspension which used upper and lower wishbones, dampers and coil springs in conjunction with an adjustable anti-roll bar. The steering was by rack and pinion mounted ahead of the front suspension. Behind the rear bulkhead (which marked the end of the driver's compartment) was the engine bay, culminating in a crossmember which carried the rear suspension.

This consisted of wishbones at the base of the uprights, top links and paired radius arms with an anti-roll bar. Once again coil springs and dampers were employed coupled with outboard disc brakes. Light alloy wheels of 15-inch front and 16-inch rear width were fitted.

A tail spoiler was tried on the car but so good was the body's shape that it merely served to slow the car down! The little coupé (only 92 inches in wheelbase and having a track of 51 inches) weighed a mere 675kg and had to carry ballast to bring it up to the minimum allowed weight of 875kg.

The Mark 6 coupé, although arriving late for the 1963 Racing Car Show at Olympia that January, was the undisputed star of the show. It was reported that Eric Broadley had gone fifty-two hours without sleep in order that the car could be displayed at the Lola stand.

It was at this time that the configuration of racing cars was undergoing a transformation. With a new generation of racing tyres by Dunlop in production, suspension systems needed good suspension control to keep the tyre as nearly vertical to the track as possible, thus maximising the usefulness of the ever increasing width of the tread.

On top of this, designers were having to investigate the shape of the bodywork as cars became faster and aerodynamics began to play an increasing part. Specifically, as racing cars (particularly sports and GT cars with their all-enveloping bodywork) began to reach speeds in excess of

The Lola Mark 6GT on display at the Racing Car Show in January 1964.

150-160mph, they began to suffer a phenomenon known as front-end lift, which showed itself to the driver as losing steering effect. This was caused by air passing underneath the car and, with an underbody shaped like an upturned aerofoil, the car's front naturally developed lift.

Rear-end lift was the opposite. In this case the car became light and twitchy as the back of the car unloaded itself at high speed. A spoiler, a thin strip of aluminium added at the upper rear across the bodywork, had been found to cure this; therefore designers reckoned that tabs added at the nose would reduce front-end lift also.

However, we are a little ahead of ourselves. The body of the new Lola had been designed to comply with the then appropriate 'GT' class, and in

May 1963 the prototype Mark 6 took part in its first race at the Silverstone International Trophy race driven by Tony Maggs.

Poor Maggs did not even have the chance to practice in the car, as John Surtees had agreed to drive it but the Ferrari team manager withdrew his consent at the last moment. Cooper works driver Maggs was forced to start from the back of the grid. Despite this impediment he finished a creditable 9th, still on the same lap as the leader. On one lap he overtook nine other cars.

The next outing was in May at the Nürburgring 1000km, where Maggs was paired with Bob Olthoff. There they retired from the race, officially after the failure of the distributor drive; unofficially, the wheel nuts kept loosening off.

The third and last international outing was in June at Le Mans. Here the drivers were Dickie Attwood (later to win the 1972 race in a Porsche 917) and David Hobbs, another English driver on an upward path. To get the car to the Sarthe circuit in time for scrutineering, Eric Broadley drove it from Dunkirk himself, thus arriving well before the transporter containing the second car. This was never used, as the arrangement for Roger Penske and Augie Pabst to drive the car collapsed, and the small Lola équipe found themselves in trouble with their own car owing to the air trunking to the carburettors being deemed to block the rear view. Also the scrutineers informed Eric Broadley that the rear bodywork was not wide enough to cover the rear tyres.

Cutaway of the Lola Mark 6GT.

Fortuitous planning meant that Peter Jackson was present with sufficient fibreglass resin and matt to remodel the rear bodywork, the trunking now taking its air from intakes mounted behind the rear side windows, and the rear wheelarches widened sufficiently to cover the rear wheels. In addition the fuel tank capacity was reduced to the specified size by inserting fourteen plastic bottles!

After delays occasioned by a slipping fan belt the Mark 6 reached 12th place by midnight. After that it fell back again with gear selector problems, until the early hours of the morning when Hobbs could not find third gear

The Lola Mark 6GT as it is today.

going into the esses and crashed. (He was fortunately unhurt.)

Ford purchased two of the three Mark 6s, made as part of its twelve-month agreement with Eric Broadley. (This was later extended by six months.) One was shipped to Dearborn for testing and evaluation and one was taken to the Goodwood Circuit in England for the same purpose. Bruce McLaren tested it at Goodwood and at Monza in November, then he prepared a very enthusiastic report for the Ford Management. In his *Autosport* column McLaren reported that the car would spin its wheels in the rain in top gear

Surtees again in the assembly area at Brands Hatch prior to the start of the race. (Courtesy LAT)

One of Eric Broadley's best-known designs: the Ford GT40 in 1968, and 1075, the winning car at Le Mans, driven by Pedro Rodriguez and Lucien Bianchi, heads towards victory. (Courtesy David Hodges)

The T53 with Dickie Attwood at South Tower corner at Crystal Palace in 1965.
(Courtesy David Hodges)

while the power available made the throttle work 'just like a tap'.

The third car had been purchased by John Mecom, a wealthy Texan with multiple interests in the oil industry (later to become Lola's agent in the USA). It was fitted with a small block Chevrolet V8 and, driven by Augie Pabst, won a race at Nassau speed week in 1965 after appearing at the 1963 Guards Trophy in England (where it retired with no oil pressure). In 1964 Augie Pabst drove it in the June sprints at Road America and the '500' event. It then went to Mosport Park and to Riverside. The car was crashed at Riverside when the throttle jammed open. Lola did make one more chassis and it is possible that the ex-Mecom car was re-chassised when it was rebuilt in later years.

During August 1963 Ford also took on John Wyer. He had a formidable reputation as the team manager of Aston Martin, culminating in their victory at Le Mans in 1959 when Carroll Shelby had shared the winning Aston Martin DBR1/300 with Roy Salvadori and second place had gone to another team car driven by Paul Frere and Maurice Trintignant.

Wyer took over as manager of the project in October 1963, and by early 1964 a new company called Ford Advanced Vehicles Limited, (FAV) had been set up in spacious factory buildings in Slough after the original Lola works had been declared too cramped.

Wyer and Broadley shared the responsibility of design and production of the Ford GT (as the new car was to be called) with the expatriate British engineer Roy Lunn. While manager of Vehicle Concepts Department at Ford in the USA, he had been heavily involved in a show-car project called 'Mustang 1'. This car bore no resemblance to the later production Mustang but was an attempt to investigate future trends.

Mustang 1 was mid-engined with the Fairlane 265cu in engine mated to the Colotti type 37 transaxle mounted in a tubular frame with independent suspension all round, side-mounted radiators and alloy body. The seats were fixed, while the pedal box was made adjustable to suit the different heights of the drivers. The oil tank, spare wheel and battery were in the nose.

The design of the new Ford GT caused problems. Roy Lunn – with a Marketing division behind him who envisaged a productionised version of the racer sometime in the future – insisted on a steel chassis. This was anathema to Eric Broadley, who wanted the car's tub fabricated in aluminium with steel bracing for light weight. Broadley even envisaged a glassfibre roof for the coupé, which did not please Lunn at all.

Events were to reach such an impasse that although the two men occupied adjoining offices they would only communicate through John Wyer, and shortly thereafter Eric Broadley decided that he wanted his works to produce cars bearing his name again and requested that his contract with Ford be renegotiated to enable this.

John Wyer and the Ford management acquiesced with regret. A mutually satisfactory parting of the ways was effected in the summer of 1964 and Lola Cars Limited set up new premises almost adjacent to FAV in Slough during the latter half of that year.

The Ford GT40 itself turned out with a steel (and therefore heavy) monocoque chassis with deep D-shaped sills, in which were housed two 140-litre bag tanks with front and rear bulkheads and the roof forming the main structure. The front and rear subframes carrying the independent suspension front and rear were also fabricated from sheet steel, and the doors were cut well into the roof to improve access. As in the Mustang concept car, the pedals and not the driver's seat were adjustable for length.

The engine was an aluminium version of the Fairlane unit fitted with four Weber carburettors and delivering 350bhp at 7200rpm. A Colotti type 37 transaxle was employed for the transmission.

The car's competition debut itself was, to say the least, unremarkable. At the Le Mans test days in April 1964 both the cars used were crashed, one by Jo Schlesser after he lost control at some 170mph on the Mulsanne straight, and one by Roy Salvadori as a result of late braking at the end of that same straight in the wet. Luckily both drivers were unhurt.

After the addition of a spoiler across the rear deck 4½ inches high, the stability of the car was vastly improved, but the Colotti gearboxes let them down at the subsequent Le Mans and Rheims races despite the great promise shown by the car.

It would take serious development both by John Wyer's team in England and Carroll Shelby's team in Venice, California to turn the car into the world-conquering endurance racer it became. In the meantime Eric Broadley had reconstituted Lola cars and had spotted gaps in the racing car market which he was quick to exploit.

T53 – 1964 – F3 – 1 built

A singleton Mark 5A (chassis number BRJ59) was rebuilt as a one-off T53 for the Midland Racing Partnership. The car itself had originally been run in Formula Two with a BRM engine, and was now re-engined with a Ford Cosworth unit mated to a four-speed Hewland transaxle.

John Blunsden tested the T53 in 1966 for *Motor Racing* and reported: 'It was a case of chasing the revs all the time, almost as though the throttle was not opening fully. Whereas on the F2 car there had been more than enough gears (six), the four permitted in F3 seemed scarcely sufficient in view of the narrower rev band of this particular unit. Also, the F3 car displayed more inherent understeer than the F2 car. The F2 car had the more desirable set-up while the F3 car, on the other hand, tended to have a little too much understeer, a condition accentuated by the lack of power.

'While this was perhaps not a completely fair comparison between F2 and F3, it served to highlight the fact that with appreciably less power the F3 car has to achieve outstanding cornering power in order to establish lap times which are not all that slower than F2 machinery. This points once again to the refining of suspensions to achieve ultimate cornering force and accepting the lack of feel that this may impart.'

T54/55 – 1964 – F2 – 7 built

When the coming of the 1000cc limit for Formula Two was announced, three Mark 5As were rebuilt for the Midland Racing Partnership to use in the formula and redesignated T54s. Richard Attwood starred in the formula against Brabham BT10s and Lotus 32s. The T54s were then subsequently rebuilt again for the MRP team, and another Mark 5A, the ex-Winkelmann car, was brought in line with T55 specification and driven with some success for the Willment team by Paul Hawkins.

John Blunsden, writing in *Motor Racing* in February 1966, wrote: 'The T54 is built around a semi-monocoque structure and, though quite heavy at 100 pounds, is still some 20-25 pounds below the F2 weight limit. The suspension units are mounted inboard at the front and controlled from the top by webbed rocking arms and the rear layout is the familiar arrangement of transverse links and trailing arms forming a wide-based double-wishbone

The wheels are shod by 5.00 and 6.00 Dunlop R6 tyres. The top panels of the Lola are in GRP by Specialised Mouldings.'

On taking to the damp track, Blunsden reported: 'I admit to feeling apprehensive during the first few laps; sooner or later it had to let go because there were too many variables affecting adhesion. Yet somehow it didn't, apart from the odd wiggle here and there under braking, and once when

set-up. The car's wheelbase is 88 inches and the track is 53 inches. The cast magnesium 13-inch wheels have 6-inch rims at the front and 8 inches at the rear. They house 10-inch and 9.5-inch Girling disc brakes, respectively.

The Formula 2 car, the T55. This is chassis number BRJ 49. (Courtesy Lola Archives)

Vallelunga 1965. The T60 in full flight. (Courtesy David Hodges)

I missed fourth gear. The moment of truth arrived when the tail went out as I was coming out of Hawthorn bend; we used a bit more track than I expected (in fact all that there was left!) but that was all. We were still pointing the right way and I felt a lot more confident – it wasn't going to swap ends just because the back wheels let go. Suddenly the car seemed to have a lot of feel to it, and although I sensed I wasn't having to concentrate so hard I knew instinctively I was motoring faster. Lola cars, through heavy preoccupation with Indy and sportscars, have not had time to fully develop the single-seaters until now. Had they done so, they would probably have given the car more ultimate cornering force but at the expense of *feel*.

It is difficult to say enough kind things about the Cosworth SCA power unit. The example fitted to the Lola must have been turning out something in the region of 120bhp, yet it has a usable power band of close to 3000rpm – all that from 999cc! Peak revs are 9800rpm but that camshaft really works from 7000rpm.'

T60/61/62 – 1965/66 – F2/F3 – 12 built

Tony Southgate, newly arrived at Lola, set about designing a monocoque chassis in conjunction with Eric Broadley for Lola's next F2 car, the T60. Eric was very tied up at this time designing the T70 and later reported the T60 as 'a most strange thing. The first one was very quick and incorporated a lot of anti-dive and anti-squat, then we built another one and it was useless!'

Despite Eric's prognosis, Chris Amon, Dickie Attwood and John Surtees all won a major F2 race in 1965 with a T60. Frank Gardner had some good outings too.

In Formula 3 in 1966 Frank Lythgoe commissioned a T60 chassis for his driver Mike Beckwith, who also had good results with it, culminating in a victory at Monza over Jonathan Williams and Chris Irwin, before switching to a Brabham as Lola failed to take much interest in F3. During 1966 the Formula Two version of the T60 was severely modified with a fuel-injected Cosworth SCA engine. In 1967 the T61 was a one-off rebuild of a Midland Racing Partnership F2 car for use by Ian Ashley in F3. Lola's T62 appeared in late 1966 and most of the cars went abroad for second-string F3 races.

Even into 1968 the T60 range showed well. John L'Amie won the Bishopscourt 1600cc Scratch Race in an ex-Robs Lamplough T62 in June, beating the Brabham of one John Watson. The T60s of Brian Nelson and Brian Cullen were both also prominent in Irish motorsport in the latter years, after the model's heyday.

T70 – 1964 – Mks 1 & 2 – 47 built

Across the Atlantic in North America, the early 1960s saw a series of races held under the auspices of the Sports Car Club of America (SCCA), which mainly consisted of wealthy amateurs driving cast-off European sports-racers such as Ferrari Testa Rossas and Maserati 300s and 450Ss mixed together with some home-built V8 specials.

Such was the popularity of these races that the SCCA started the United States Road Racing Championship (USRRC) in 1963 in order to award big prize money and therefore bring top drivers and cars from all over the world to compete with one another.

In 1962 a very bright young racer called Roger Penske had seen a way to beat the established opposition when he purchased a crashed F1 Cooper T53 from Briggs Cunningham's racing team. His mechanic, Roy Gaine, modified the car with all-enveloping bodywork and, with Penske at the wheel, it promptly showed a clean set of wheels to opponents at Riverside and Laguna Seca.

Naturally the car was banned by the American racing authorities, and the 'Zerex Special', as it was named,

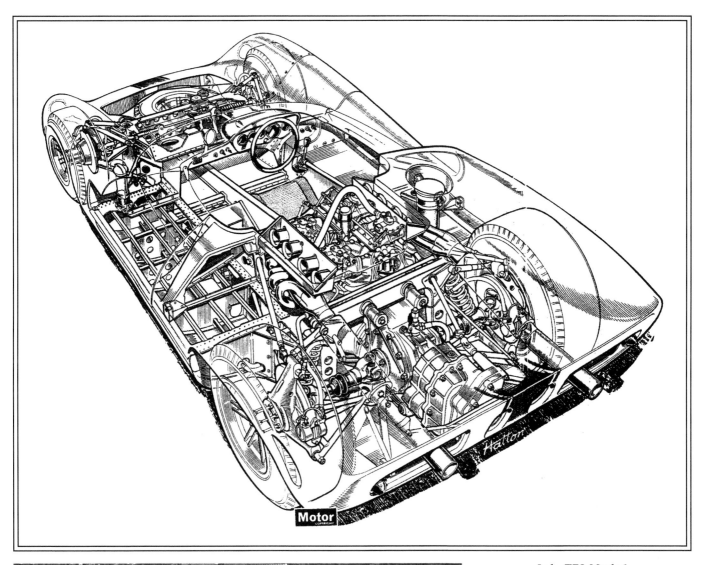

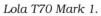

Lola T70 Mark 1.

Left: John Surtees and the winning Lola T70 Mark 2 (SL71-16) after winning the Guards International Trophy at Brands Hatch in 1965. Alongside him is Denny Hulme and in the car is the actor, Patrick McGoohan! (Courtesy David Cundy)

was sold to John Mecom, who had it reworked to a more normal side-by-side seating configuration to conform to the rules concerning passenger space. The resultant car was then driven to further success by Penske in America. It came to England and won the Guards Trophy at Brands Hatch in 1963. Bruce McLaren saw the potential, bought the car and replaced the Climax 2.7-litre engine with a 3.5-litre aluminium Oldsmobile V8.

Now with more power, and Bruce driving, the car achieved many wins, repeating its Guards Trophy win of the year before, ahead of the Lotus 30 designed and put into limited production by Colin Chapman to accommodate the Ford 289-cu in V8 engine.

Around this time, the FIA, realising the groundswell of change which these

The Lola T70 Mark 2 at its launch at the Racing Car Show in January 1966. (Author's collection)

Anglo-American hybrids were bringing in to sportscar racing, re-organised the categories of cars which could compete in International races. Groups 1-4 were allocated to production cars while Groups 5 and 6 were for small production runs. Groups 7-9 were for, respectively, Formula racing cars and Formula Libre racing cars, and the FIA, under pressure from the American federation and the RAC, added Group 9 (under Category 'C' for racing cars) specifically for '2-seater racers'. It was obvious that these big American-engined sports-racers were the coming thing both in the UK and the US, and Eric Broadley introduced the T70 to sell to this market.

In January 1965 the result of his small company's labours was to be seen when the new Lola T70 was displayed at the Racing Car Show in London. It was the star of the exhibition. Beneath the beautifully shaped glass reinforced plastic (GRP) body by Peter Jackson's Specialised Mouldings, the chassis was all that Roy Lunn had *not* allowed Eric Broadley to produce.

The central structure was a sheet steel floor extending sideways to encompass D-shaped sills on either side which did not use bag tanks. Instead, to save weight, aluminium fuel tanks were hung from the steel sides and fastened top and bottom with flanges. Thirty-two gallons of fuel could be carried.

The slope of the rear bulkhead formed the back of the driving compartment to which the driver's seat was fitted, and the the rear tub sides embraced the engine which was a semi-stressed member. The length of this 'bathtub' type chassis, incidentally, was 93½ inches. The new Hewland LG (Large Gearbox) 500 (the amount of horsepower the box could handle) four-speed gearbox was used. This gearbox featured a detachable rear cover which enabled all ratios to be changed in as little as thirty minutes and, with a magnesium casing, only weighed 125 pounds. This was surrounded by two rear castings top and bottom from which the suspension took its pick-up points.

At the front the pedal box was enclosed, while two radiators and the mandatory spare wheel were supported in the GRP nose – although from chassis SL70/7 the nose was made detachable and a box-shaped fabrication from aluminium now supported the radiators.

The airflow from the radiators was ducted out through the top of the nose, thus giving some useful downforce, and the rear of the bodywork was quickly detachable via pip pins.

Probably the most unusual feature of the design was the brakes. These were mounted inboard of the fifteen-inch diameter by eight-inch front (and the same diameter) by ten-inch wide rear wheels to provide better cooling for the solid iron discs which were retarded by single piston calipers.

The front suspension employed top and bottom wishbones connected to a magnesium upright with Armstrong coil and damper units and six-stud fixings for wheel location. BMC rack and pinion steering (from the Austin 1100) was used. At the rear, inverted wishbones were used at the bottom, while at the top a single link sufficed, with twin radius rods on each side, to locate the entire suspension. The rear anti-roll bar acted on the top links, whereas the front one acted on the lower wishbones.

Another view of the Lola T70 on display at the Racing Car Show.

pounds the car was too heavy and was already designing the Mark 2 as a lighter version.

The tub of the Mark 2 used 85 per cent aluminium alloy with only 15 per cent sheet steel, as compared to 60 per cent steel for the earlier car. Riveted construction now took the

Front brake of SL70/1 whilst being built in the factory.

Wheelbase was 95 inches and track 54 inches. Broadley had designed the T70 to take any American stock block engine up to six litres and the show model sported a 4.5-litre Oldsmobile V8.

John Surtees had gone into partnership with Lola to form Team Surtees, virtually a works team, and the first car (SL70/1) went to him, painted bright red with green longitudinal stripes. In initial testing the car proved phenomenally fast, soon beating the Formula One lap record at most circuits – witness 1 minute 36.6 seconds at Oulton Park in May, 1.2 seconds lower than the F1 lap record. Even so, Surtees requested more power still and progressed through the season via a 5-litre Chevrolet to a 5.9-litre version (all tuned by the American Traco concern), which put out some 550bhp on high-octane fuel.

Other noteworthy drivers of the Mark 1 were David Hobbs (driving Harold Young's SL70/2), Walt Hansgen (driving John Mecom's cars), Hugh Dibley (driving Stirling Moss's car, SL70/4, afterwards re-chassised with tub number SL70/7) and Carroll Shelby (acting as a team owner with SL70/10).

Although some fifteen cars were made, Broadley knew that at 1375

Hugh Dibley's T70 Mark 1 in 1966 at Brands Hatch.
(Courtesy Lola Collection)

place of the welding used on Mark 1. According to the factory this saved seventy pounds in weight alone.

Fuel bags giving an increase in capacity to fifty gallons were now inserted into the sponsons, as the previous design had led to leaks with the distortion of

Eric Broadley in his epochal Mark 6 GT car, probably at Silverstone.

41

*David Hobbs in T70 Mark 1,
S170/2, at Oulton Park in 1965.*

the sponsons in racing, and now no less than three Bendix fuel pumps were used. The wheel widths were quoted at eight inches front and ten inches rear. Cooling was taken care of via a single radiator with an oil cooler incorporated. This was made possible as the Group 9 rules had been changed so that a spare wheel no longer needed to be carried – thus freeing up space in the nose section.

The bodywork saved thirty-five pounds in weight by not being colour impregnated, and the factory advised as little paint as possible to be applied. Discs were radially ventilated to improve cooling, while the rear suspension radius arms were moved more inboard to bring them directly in line with the suspension mountings.

A typical example (SL71/38) was delivered to Jackie Epstein on 26 August 1966 and featured an Alan Smith (of Derby) tuned Chevrolet, knock-off hubs and Armstrong dampers. Tyres were Firestone Indy 9.20-15 front and 12.00-15 rear, and front and rear spoilers were fitted.

*Nigel Hulme in a Lola T70 Mark 1 when racing SL70/13 in historic events.
(Courtesy David Hodges)*

Denny Hulme awaits the start of a race at Silverstone in Sid Taylor's Mark 2 in 1966. (Author's collection)

Driving the new Mark 2, Surtees showed it to be appreciably faster than the original cars and won the Guards International Trophy at Brands Hatch in the new Team Surtees car, chassis number SL71/16. The gap to second-place Bruce McLaren was over ninety seconds but Bruce was to learn many lessons and would eventually humble the Lola T70s in the championship they were destined to compete in first of all: the Can-Am series.

Meanwhile in England in June 1966 the RAC had announced that Group 7 racing was to be cancelled from the end of the season through lack of interest. Could this have had something to do with the RAC favouring Formula Two at the time?

SL71/16 was, incidentally, written off in Surtees' huge accident at Mosport Park in practice for the Pepsi 100. Thanks to two marshals on the spot, Surtees survived a series of horrendous end-over-end flips, although the accident put him out of racing until the middle of 1966. The remains of number 16 were buried at Mosport.

1965 racing

With the FIA and CSI (FISA's forerunner) adopting the Sports Car Club of America's rules and calling them Group 9 in 1965, the way was now open for racing these new 'hairy monsters' for the first time on both sides of the Atlantic. Bruce McLaren, after buying Roger Penske's 'Zerex Special' and modifying it still further, produced what was called a McLaren Elva Oldsmobile, while Colin Chapman had introduced his Lotus 40 – a development of the Lotus 30 – to race in these events. This had a

John Surtees at Riverside in the CanAm race of 1966 when he won the championship.

Roger Penske's 'Sunoco Special' T70, as it is today.

Ford V8 engine of 4.7 litres from their experimental department and, to handle the increased 'urge' of this engine, Lotus replaced the ZF gearbox of the Type 30 with a Hewland 4-speed LG500. Girling, in conjunction with Lotus, came up wih a three-pad caliper design along with ventilated discs, and stronger uprights, radius arms and wishbones were fitted.

Both these Lotus designs developed reputations as ill-handling monsters – even the great Jim Clark had trouble keeping them on the track – and with the advent of the well-mannered, good-handling Lola T70, the Type 30 was relegated to the also-rans. The McLaren-designed line of Group 7 cars was, however, another matter and they were destined to provide Lola with their stiffest opposition in the years to come.

Straight away the Lola started embarrassing the current Formula One designs. At Silverstone it was no less than one-and-a-half seconds faster than the Grand Prix lap record at 1:31.0. By June Surtees had taken his big red

T70 around in 1:28.3 and the promoters were concerned about the Formula One fans turning out to watch Group 7/9 cars instead. Perhaps this was one of the reasons that races for Group 7 cars were dropped from the British calender at the end of 1966.

On 20 March at Silverstone John Surtees, the development driver for Lola, led his race easily until falling back just three laps from home with mechanical problems. He finished second to Jim Clark in the works Lotus 30. Surtees then took the car to America for the Players 200 at Mosport Park and, with an easy victory, really showed the SCCA regulars what the new British design could do.

In England David Hobbs had taken the second car (so new that it raced unpainted) to a third-place finish at Goodwood in April, ahead of BOAC Airline pilot Hugh Dibley in his new Lola but behind Jim Clark in the Lotus and Bruce McLaren in his McLaren Elva Oldsmobile. Hobbs then took second place in the Tourist Trophy at Oulton

Roger McClusky tries the T70 Spyder for size during the USRRC series in 1965.

Mark Donohue driving one of Roger Penske's T70 Mark 2s in the CamAm series of 1965.

Park in May, behind Denny Hulme in a two-litre Brabham BT8. At last, Hobbs drove to victory on 7 June in the Guards Trophy at Mallory Park, a race held over two heats (the winner having the best result on aggregate).

Back in England for the Martini Trophy race at Silverstone on 24 July, Surtees took pole but did not finish the race. Neither did Hugh Dibley, for his gearbox failed while he was lying second after twenty four laps.

Probably the most notable victory yet for the new T70 was in the Guards International Trophy at Silverstone on 30 August, where John Surtees won in the first Mark 2 with a ninety second lead ahead of Bruce McLaren, with Jackie Stewart coming third in the very first T70 made. However, Pierpoint, Hobbs and Dibley all retired their Lolas, while Walt Hansgen, in the second Mark 2 built, finished ninth.

David Hobbs now joined the money trail in America in September at Mont Tremblant-St Jovite, to come third overall while Surtees took the victory.

The following week John Surtees suffered a huge accident at Mosport in practice. A hub carrier broke while he was exiting turn one, and the T70 vaulted over the guard-rail and shot down a nearby embankment. John Surtees was lucky to survive, and it was not until 1966 that he was racing again.

John Mecom had become the Lola agent in North America and he used Walt Hansgen as his driver in SCCA races in SL70/6. Hansgen turned in some fine performances, winning the races at Laguna Seca (taking home $40,000 in prize money) and Monterey and coming second at Las Vegas in the Stardust Grand Prix. Mecom used his oil millions to build himself some very impressive premises near Houston International Airport, making many parts for the T70s he purchased from Lola. His house-built engines sported aluminium blocks and huge side-draught 58mm Weber carburettors.

After building his own V8-powered car, the Attila Chevrolet, Roy Pierpont took David Good's T70 to South Africa where it lasted six of the Kyalami nine hours until the engine broke. Paul Hawkins then drove this car in the Cape International three hours at Killarney. It was to be his first race of many in a Lola T70.

Bob Bondurant in a Mark 1 T70 during the 1966 CanAm. Note the oval ducts which gather air for the side-mounted 58mm Weber carburettors (an arrangement also used on Mark Donohue's car), and, beside it, the cooling air scoop on the gearbox.

5

1966-1967

T80/90 – 1965/66/67 – USAC/Indy – 9 built

Eric Broadley saw the example set by Lotus at Indianapolis in 1963 and 1964, and realised the large amounts of start, sponsor and prize money to be gained there. Using particularly his inside knowledge of the Ford Fairlane engine he had utilised in the Mark 6, he wasted little time in coming up with the first of his cars for racing at the Hoosier bowl, the T80.

Typically, the T80 was a combined steel and aluminium 'bathtub' with the suspension being offset to help with adhesion on the bankings as was the case with the typical American racer of the period.

The T80 was powered by the new Ford four-cam engine (basically new twin-cam heads, Offenhauser of the period, on the aluminium Fairlane-type block,) and driving through a ZF gearbox. It was sold to A J Foyt, Parnelli Jones and Bud Tinglestadt. Surprisingly they did not shine in the 1965 event, Foyt and Jones driving Lotus's, but Al Unser did come in ninth in the 'Sheraton Thompson Special' T80 as a member of Foyt's team. Tingelstadt started twenty-fourth in the 'American Red Ball Special' and was classified sixteenth after losing a wheel and hitting the wall.

For 1966 Lola introduced the T90, now with an all-aluminium monocoque chassis (most people still refer to 'tub', as in 'bathtub' when describing monocoque construction) and a two-speed Hewland gearbox but with the same suspension as the previous year. At the model's debut

Gasoline Alley, Indianapolis 1965. A J Foyt sits in the new T80 with, on his right, the legendary George Bignotti and, in hat, Martin Buckley. Just look at that suspension stagger! (Courtesy Indianapolis Motor Speedway)

Graham Hill driving the Red Ball Special Lola T90 to victory during the 1966 Indianapolis 500.
(Courtesy David Hodges)

at the 20 March season opener at Phoenix International, Roger Ward came in second overall. Two months later, on 24 June, Ward scored Lola's first Indycar race at Trenton just before that year's Indianapolis 500.

All three cars at the Indianapolis 500 were entered by John Mecom and tended to by the legendary American race engineer George Bignotti. With less than twenty-five miles to go, Jackie Stewart led Graham Hill in what looked

Inset: The Lola T90 at the works before despatch to Indianapolis for the 1966 event. (Courtesy David Hodges)

Graham Hill shaking hands with Earl B Hathaway, president of Firestone Tyre Company, after Graham won the 1966 Indianapolis 500 race, beating Jim Clark and Jim McElreath in the process. (Courtesy Firestone Tyres)

as if it would be a Lola 1-2, but Stewart's engine failed and Graham Hill motored on in the 'Red Ball Special' to Lola's first 'Brickyard' win. It would not be their last ... Jackie Stewart was still classified sixth, such had been his lead, but Roger Ward in the 'Bryant Heating

Firestone tyres gave me Championship performance & safety in winning this 500 mile race Graham Hill

Graham Hill poses in the winning Lola T90 and dedicates his victory to Firestone Tyres.
(Author's collection)

The F2 Lola with the Apfelbeck-headed BMW engine at Jarama in 1967. (Courtesy David Hodges)

The Lola T102 BMW of Hubert Hahne at Jarama in 1969. (Courtesy David Hodges)

Special' Lola, fitted with an Offenhauser engine, failed to finish.

For 1967 the T92, actually the original T90 rebuilt, was deemed a sufficient development with its symmetrical suspension to carry on in Indy racing, and indeed Stewart was in line to take second place – when his engine let go again at the Indianapolis 500. Despite a last lap accident, Chuck Hulse was classified seventh in the 'Hopkins Special' T92 using a turbocharged Offy.

T100 – 1967/69 – F2 – 9 built
Lola's final Formula Two car, the

T100, featured the now mandatory monocoque construction but with torsion bar suspension, adjustable anti-roll bars and Koni dampers, and was raced primarily by Team Surtees with 'Big John' and Chris Irwin doing most of the driving and taking many victories.

Most T100s were Cosworth FVA-engined, although some sported the BMW Apfelbeck headed engine which had been designed by Paul Rosche and which, though powerful, proved to be unreliable. BMW enlisted the services of Jo Siffert and Hubert Hahne to drive their cars with Kurt Ahrens

Jacky Ickx in the F2 Lola BMW of 1970. (Courtesy David Hodges)

The Lola T102 F2 car of 1970. (Courtesy David Hodges)

Friday, leaving Chris Irwin to drive the BMW version. Hahne was in the BMW car but all three retired. On Easter Monday, Siffert drove another BMW-engined car but retired in the first heat with fuel injection problems; John Surtees finished third on the aggregate of two heats to the Brabham BT23s of Jochen Rindt and Alan Rees. One month later Surtees was beaten by Rindt again, this time at the Nürburgring in atrocious conditions of ice and snow. A BMW-engined car had been Surtees' mount on this occasion, Hahne finished fourth and Irwin, in the FVA-engined Lola, was seventh.

John Surtees reverted to the FVA-engined car on 14 May to win the Guards Trophy at Mallory Park by an astonishing three laps from Frank Gardner in a BT23. One week later and Surtees won again, this time at Zolder.

David Bridges of the Red Rose team from Lancashire ordered one for his driver, Brian Redman, who did equally well, although he crashed on the car's debut at Hockenheim when his clutch failed. In September Brian came in sixth at Albi and was fourth at the Vallelunga finale to claim ninth in the overall title battle while Irwin was sixth. It is possible that John Surtees' involvement with the T70 and the Formula One cars blunted their team's success in the Formula Two title chase.

standing in when Siffert was racing F1 or Sportscars.

John Surtees drove the FVA-engined car at Snetterton for the first round of the Championship on Good

Other drivers who impressed in rare outings in a T100 were David Hobbs and Chris Williams, while John Watson, using a Ford twin-cam engine, scored worthwhile results later in the 1960s.

In 1968 Alister Walker, Robin Widdows and Chris Williams campaigned their T100s, with Chris Irwin winning at the Nürburgring and placing third at Zolder; Chris was later badly injured at the Nürburgring in the Ford F3L sports prototype and retired from racing.

Also in 1968 two T102s were built up by BMW personnel at the Slough factory. These were similar to the T100 but featured a tubular engine bay and lighter alloys all the way through the main structure and in the suspension. Their debut was at Hockenheim in October, driven by Siffert and Hahne. Siffert led from Hahne to begin with but then became entangled with others and retired with suspension damage. Hahne was seventh but Hobbs came in fifth, only 2.2 seconds behind the winning Ferrari of Brambilla.

For 1969 BMW reverted to their M12 sixteen-valve engine in the T102 to replace the Apfelbeck engine. Now the cars featured large rear wings which feathered automatically when fifth gear was selected; Hahne and Siffert scored several second places between them during the year but overall success eluded them.

6
1968-1969

T120 – 1968 – Group 7 – 1 built

The T110 was a stillborn project for a Formula One car which did not materialize; the T120 was something of a throwback, featuring a spaceframe for a one-off sports/racing car commissioned for BMW to run in Group 7 in the European Mountain Championship.

Dieter Quester came in third with it at Ollon-Villars and Gaisberg, beaten only by the Porsches of Gerhard Mitter and Rolf Stommelen. Later on, Quester won at both the Vienna and Innsbruck courses in October, and he was placed second overall in the 1968 Mountain Championship. In July Dieter Quester had raced the T120 and proved a sensation at the Norisring during two 100-mile heats, coming in second overall to David Piper's Ferrari P4 and beating all the Porsche 910s.

T130 – 1968 – F1 – 1 built

Actually built up in Team Surtees workshops and named as the Honda RA300, the T130 was a combined effort featuring Honda's V12 engine, Team Surtees' know-how and Lola's design expertise.

Some components came directly from the Indy T90, specifically the tub which was the same up to the rear bulkhead, after which it was adapted to take the Honda engine. The car scored a debut victory at Monza where John Surtees drove it to win the Italian Grand Prix. Suspension was typical of Lola cars at this period, double wishbone at the front with reversed lower wishbones at the rear and a transverse upper link with radius arms locating the whole assembly.

Dieter Quester hustles the T120 up a hillclimb in Europe, 1967.
(Courtesy Lola Archives)

The Lola T180 F1 car with Honda V12 engine. (Courtesy Honda Motor Corporation)

T140/142 – 1968 – A/5000 – 45 built

During the winter of 1967-1968 Lola suffered many cancellations of its T70 design due to the CSI's introduction of its 50-off homologation ruling for the Group 4 category, thus placing the future of the beautiful coupé in jeopardy. Fortunately the CSI recanted enough to allow Lola to count in the Spyder versions of their T70 to make up the necessary number but, casting around for something to do with the already bought-in components such as brakes, uprights, etc, Lola displayed true inventiveness and designed a single-seater spaceframe chassis for Formula 5000 to take mainly T70 components.

The Italian Grand Prix, held at Monza in 1968, and John Surtees in the T180/Honda duels with a works Ferrari. (Courtesy Honda Motor Corporation)

Called the T140 for Formula Atlantic (and later, with some modifications for 1969 and European F5000, the T142) the new category of FA/5000 with big, mainly Chevrolet, five-litre engines was catered for. No one could call the T140 beautiful, but it was certainly effective. Jerry Hansen scored his once-only SCCA FA victory in a Lola 1-2-3 debut at Elkhart Lake at the beginning of July.

Both Roger Penske and Sid Taylor bought T142s for their teams but, the T140 found itself up against more sophisticated opposition in the shape of monocoque structured McLarens, Surtees and Eagles; indeed, Eagles finished 1-2 in the FA Championship, driven by Lou Sell and George Wintersteen. Ex-Lola designer Tony Southgate had designed the Eagles ...

For 1969 Tony Lanfranchi took the first T142 to Brands Hatch and shattered the short circuit lap record by 1.2 seconds to delight Sid Taylor, the car's new owner. At Silverstone on the 16 May T142s finished first (Mike Walker), third (Willie Forbes), fourth (Ulf Norinder) and sixth (Keith Holland). Probably their finest hour was at Oulton Park on 20 September when T142s filled the first six places and Mike Walker was again the victor. One week later Mike Hailwood won the Guards Trophy Finale at Brands Hatch in Chassis Number SL142/40. Jackie Epstein, Hailwood's team manager, remembered: 'We had a lot of engine

trouble, and that's what finally decided us to go about engines another way. We were running wet-sump engines which surged and caused the bearings to get hot and the crankshaft to twist. It was at Mallory Park where we had our last engine failure on that first batch of engines and it was on the day Paul Hawkins was killed at Oulton Park.

'After that Eric asked me to continue running the F5000 car, so with Nick Cuthbert – who had actually owned Paul's T70 – we continued. Eric Broadley had supplied the chassis, mechanic, workshop, etc. and Nick now supplied the engines which were

modified and maintained by Lola. We were third in the Championship, although Mike only won one race. He drove extremely well, the T142 being much to his liking as it was a consistent oversteerer. It suffered from inadequate shock absorbers and at peak sideways G suffered from a lack of chassis stiffness, too. It was, of course, technically outclassed by the McLaren M10A and the Surtees TS5.'

Eddy Weitzes won all five rounds of the Canadian FA Championship; second was the similar car of Horst Kroll. Later on Carlos Avallone of Brazil took his crashed T142 back to Brazil,

Mike Walker at Oulton Park in a T142 in 1969. (Courtesy David Hodges)

60

rebodied it with T222 Can-Am bodywork and won a race at Sao Paulo.

T150/152/153/154 – 1968/69/70 – Indy – 7 built

Lola's next design for Indianapolis-type racing, after the T92, was the T150, a very advanced car utilising four-wheel drive by Hewland. It featured the by now usual monocoque, and was wider than most USAC cars, with a distinct wedge-shaped nose. The T150 was produced in conjunction with Hewland in 1968 with the option of two- or four-wheel drive. The original idea was to sort it out properly in two-wheel drive trim, then switch to four-wheel drive, thereby not blaming the four-wheel drive system for any problems which might arise which were in fact inherent in the basic design of the car. In fact, the fwd system as developed by Mike Hewland proved very good; it owed much to the previous Ferguson system,

having a DG main casing, gear cluster and crownwheel, but it also featured a new rear end casing which side-stepped the drive to the right from where a propshaft ran to an LG differential which was offset and took the drive to the front of the car. Mike Hewland had designed the system to cope with a Ford four-camshaft engine giving less than 500bhp and was concerned when he found that a 700bhp turbocharged engine would be used instead – but he need not have worried.

The T152 was the 1969 model and the T153/154 was a two-wheel drive version for 1970, after fwd had been outlawed by USAC. The first car built was for Al Unser, then two more were constructed for Roger Penske's team for Mark Donohue to drive.

In 1968 the only Lola in the Indy 500 was the new T150 fwd of Al Unser, who started sixth after qualifying at 167.069mph and was still running in

sixth position when he hit the wall, and was therefore classified twenty-sixth with forty laps completed.

First, second and fourth places went to the Eagles designed by former Lola man Tony Southgate, and Bobby Unser won at a new record speed with two-wheel drive after the turbine-powered Lotus cars of Art Pollard and Lloyd Ruby had both retired within a few laps of the finish with gearbox mainshaft failure.

This win also marked the return to prominence of the turbocharged Offenhauser engine after three straight Ford wins. Later in the season, in July and immediately following a dirt track win at Nazareth in a Roger Ward-entered Offy, Al Unser won double victories on consecutive weekends at the 1968 Hoosier 100 and then the Langhorne twins in a T150 fwd. But it was not enough to wrest the USAC title away from Bobby Unser who, on 4330 points,

The T150 four wheel drive Indianapolis car built for the Roger Penske/Sunoco team in 1969. (Courtesy David Hodges)

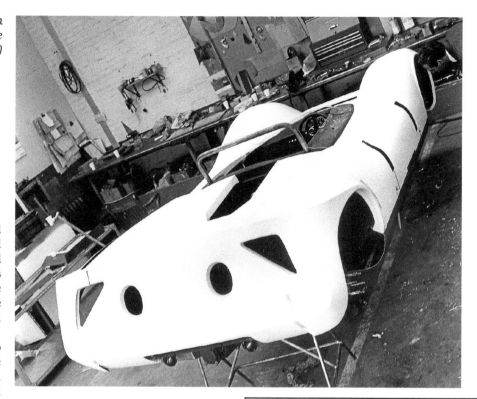

T160; the second part of the CanAm effort. The almost-finished car at the factory in 1968. (Courtesy LAT)

was the champion, with Mario Andretti second on 4319. Al Unser came third with 2895. Incidentally, four-wheel drive was banned at the Indianapolis 500 from 1 January 1970 despite reports from Harry Ferguson and the likes of Al Unser that it was safer than two-wheel drive systems.

In 1969 Bobby Unser switched to Lola and was third at Indy while rookie Mark Donohue was seventh, both in four-wheel drive T152s. Andretti won with a Brawner Hawk Ford, really a copy of a Lotus. Al Unser had been injured in a motor cycle accident and was replaced in the VPJ Offy T152 fwd by Bud Tingelstad who was classified 15th. It was the last outing of four-wheel drive at Indy, but a close copy of the two-wheel drive T152, the Colt, won the race in 1970 and 1972, driven on both occasions by Al Unser.

Al won three races for Lola in 1969, the Milwaukee 200 in August, at Kent Raceway in October and the Phoenix 200 in November. He also won twice more, on dirt, in a King Ford. Mario Andretti took the title with 5025 points, Al was next on 2630 and Bobby Unser third on 2585.

The 1970 season saw Mark Donohue place second at Indy in a T154 (the only pukka Lola to compete that year) behind Al Unser's 'Johnny Lightning Special', the Lola-based P J Colt of Parnelli Jones. Joe Leonard was twenty-fourth in another 'JLS' Colt after covering 73 laps out of the 200. Colts also won at Phoenix, Milwaukee (twice), Indianapolis Raceway Plaza and Trenton to help give Al the USAC title over brother Bobby in an Eagle.

Al Unser won the Indy 500 again in 1970 in the 'Johnny Lightning Special' P J Colt. David Hobbs came in twentieth on 107 laps out of 200 in the same Penske T154 with which had come second in the previous year. Sam Sessions finished twenty-seventh in an Agajanian-entered Lola.

Al Unser was beaten into fourth place in the championship despite winning both races at the Rafaela opener in Argentina, and then at Phoenix, before missing out to Mike Mosley in an Eagle at Trenton. He then won Indy and Milwaukee straight off, making it five from six. However, he scored no more wins in the final six events, and Joe Leonard in a Colt took the crown with a singleton victory at Ontario and 3016 points, then came Foyt with one win and 2320, Billy Vukovich Jr with no wins and 2250, and Al Unser five wins and 2220 points.

In 1972 Sam Sessions came fourth and Wally Dallenbach fifteenth in new Lola T270s. Mark Donohue won for McLaren from the Parnellis of Al Unser and Joe Leonard.

Cutaway drawing of the T160 of 1968.

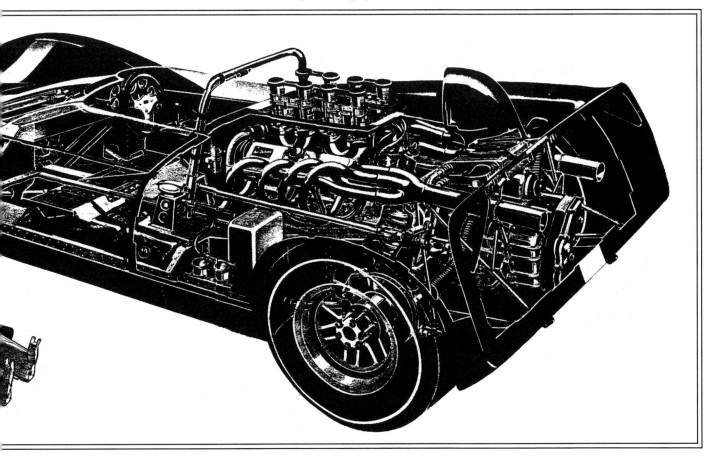

John Saphir in the Hannibal Racing Lola T160 at Brands Hatch in 1988. (Courtesy David Cundy)

CanAm, Bridgehampton, 1968, and John Surtees pilots his own TS-Chevrolet T160. (Courtesy David Hodges)

T160/162/163 – 1968/70 – Gp 7 Can-Am – 25 built

In 1968 Eric Broadley realized that to combat the McLarens in the rich Can-Am series he would need more power, and the only way to achieve that in the American market was to utilise the new 'big block' Chevrolet engine of 427 cubic inches, the immortal seven-litre.

In addition, the T70 Mark 3 had some disadvantages, primarily the one-piece rear bulkhead which supported the rear suspension. Changing an engine was laborious and took a long time – something which detachable top and bottom crossmembers would make a lot simpler. More torsional rigidity and general simplifying would not go amiss either. It is important to realize that through all of this period racing cars were growing ever more powerful, wheel rim widths were growing almost by the day, and slick tyres were starting to be introduced; the car which had the stiffest chassis and the suspension best able to utilise these colossal changes would be king.

First tested in May 1968 by John Surtees, the T160 was more angular than the T70 it superseded. Also the T160 was almost two and a half times stiffer even though its bare weight was a mere 130 pounds with a simpler

The Lola T180's Honda engine being worked on. The detail photos are of the front and rear suspension. (Courtesy LAT)

The Lola T180/Honda F1 car with Surtees at the wheel. (Courtesy LAT)

Honest, Officer, it's road legal! A T160 when owned by Rod Leach of Nostalgia fame. (Courtesy Rod Leach)

and lighter tub skinned in 16-gauge aluminium.

The Mark 3B T70 coupé of 1969 would feature an almost identical tub. The suspension members followed the then current Lola practice with steel wishbone tubes brazed onto the sockets of the lower ball joints with both balls in the uprights, and rose joints at the front upper and rear lower inboard mountings to permit camber and castor adjustment. Dampers were Koni double adjustable, and adjustable anti-roll bars were, as usual, in use at the front and rear. Twelve-inch diameter by 1.1 inches thick ventilated discs with alloy calipers made in four pieces (each caliper having four brake pads) were mounted outboard all round, unlike the T140/142 Formula 5000 car, and a big block Chevrolet of seven litres was

T160 with bodywork removed and a later small block engine fitted. (Courtesy Rod Leach)

John Surtees cornering hard with the T180/Honda in the Italian Grand Prix of 1968. (Courtesy David Hodges)

installed. John Surtees' own engine used Weslake heads.

Whatever the engine choice, a Hewland LG600 five-speed and reverse gearbox was fitted (the '600' denoted how many horsepower the gearbox could cope with), and oil coolers for both gearbox and engine were mounted at the rear, above the gearbox. Two rubber fuel tank bags held a total of fifty gallons and fed a collector tank situated just in front of the left rear wheelarch. The dry-sump oil tank

was situated on the other side of the chassis, and gearbox and engine oil cooler were placed, one on top of the other, over the gearbox.

Wheel sizes were 15-inch diameter by 9-inch wide fronts and 14-inch rears (although this measurement would swiftly become 17 inches). Bodywork, as usual with Lola products, was by Specialised Mouldings, and the wheelbase was 94 inches, front track 56 inches and rear track 51 inches (depending on rim size); weight

was given as 1,450 pounds and its distribution was 40/60 front/rear. Dan Gurney and James Garner of AIR both ordered T160s for the Can-Am series, while John Surtees bought one car, took it back to his own Team Surtees facility and extensively reworked it, renaming it the 'TS-Chevrolet'.

Back in 1968 the T160 was still unable to overcome the McLaren steamroller. The new Can-Am car was disappointing that year due to a lack of development following Surtees'

Below: Mike Hailwood in the Lola T190 entered by Jackie Epstein. Hailwood enjoyed many successful races in the Formula 5000 series. (Courtesy David Hodges)

departure. The best results were courtesy of the Simoniz cars (SL160-9) driven by Chuck Parsons (race number 10), who gained a fifth at Edmonton and a fourth in the Stardust finale at Las Vegas, where Follmer's T70 was second. Mario Andretti and Sam Posey/Skip Scott also piloted T160s (Simoniz-sponsored race number 26, SL160-2, sold later to Jerry Weichers and now owned by Stewart Hall of California), as did David 'Swede' Savage in Gurney's team car, but at the end of the season, the T160 was only tenth in the points. John Surtees' own car was a disappointment, but this was down to the Weslake-headed engine, which failed in each of his three races.

SL160-9 was later used as a road car by a doctor in South Carolina, and by Rod Leach, owner of 'nostalgia', who specialised in selling exotic cars. SL160-12 was owned for many years by Dan Martin and then sold to Sweden. It now has a new owner in America.

Only two T162 developments were built, chassis numbers SL162-13 and 14. The chassis was identical to the T70 Mark 3B then being designed; in fact, all mechanical parts are interchangeable between the two designs. SL162-13 was raced at one time by Monte Shelton and then sold to Tom Armstrong of Washington, while SL162-14 was campaigned by Bob Dini and crashed at St Jovite. The car sat in New York for twenty years until it was purchased by Jerry Weichers in 1989. The tub was rebuilt by Harold Drinkwater and the car was sold again to Tom Coburn of California.

Hailwood again in the T190, this time at Thruxton. (Courtesy David Hodges)

Both the T162 and the T163 sported modifications to the suspension and body shape in an attempt to get on terms with the McLarens; in this they failed, but then so did everyone else in the Can-Am until the advent of the Porsche 917/10 in the 1970s. The T163, additionally, had modifications made to the bulkheads and fuel bags.

For 1969 the most successful regular driver was Chuck Parsons, whose lightweight T163 – powered now by a Chaparral built Chevvy – placed third overall in 1969 as the best of the rest behind the Kiwis (who had eight 1-2 results in their McLarens in ten events). Parsons was second at Riverside and third at St Jovite and Laguna Seca. Other T163 drivers were Ronnie Bucknum and Peter Revson, sharing the same car, and Mark Donohue in a Penske car

In 1970 Dave Causey was fourth in the points in a T165. A mid-season flourish saw him gain a third place at Road America followed up with a second at Road Atlanta. His was the first Lola behind the Hulme, Motschenbacher and Gethin McLaren M8Ds.

Today, most of the T160s have survived and several have been re-bodied with T70 coupé bodies, notably SL160/1 and SL163/18 with a Mark 3 body, but it is reasonable to suppose that with the ever-increasing spread of historic racing these will sooner or later be taken back to their original form. Indeed, Craig Bennet in the USA races a T163 which is regularly the class of the field in the popular Can-Am 'Vintage' races held there.

T180 – 1968 – F1 (Honda) – 1 built
The car was publicly designated the Honda RA301. It was a full length monocoque with very similar suspension to RA300, yet it is reported that it was designed by Mr Sano – and there were two of them! (Could the second one have been a modified RA300?). Sadly, the R301 was heavier than the RA300.

John Surtees used the 'old' V8 instead of the new V12 to take second place in the 1968 French Grand Prix, its best result, but ironically Jo Schlesser was in the same race and was killed in the new RA302. Later John Surtees took third place in the US Grand Prix, but Honda quit at the end of the season.

An interview with Surtees and bossman Yoshio Nakamura in Autosport confirmed that the chassis was made in England while the engine and gearbox came from Japan. Arch Motors made the wishbones, etc. The car was built using the facilities of both Lola and Honda, and the car's design was said to be a combination of Eric Broadley, Yoshio Nakamura and Mr Sano ...

The 'Hondola' was white with red stripes – no Surtees arrow was in evidence – and its first Grand Prix appearance was at Spain in 1968. It was in third place late on when the gear linkage came apart. It was one hundred pounds lighter than before and had a wheelbase two inches shorter than the Monza winner (which was itself three inches shorter than the earlier V12s).

The RA301 had been first tested at Suzuka. Honda Racing was now completely run by Team Surtees in Slough, thus avoiding commuting of people and transport parts to and from Japan.

T190/190X/192 – 1969/71 – FA/ F5000 – 20 built
The T190 monocoque superseded the spaceframe F5000 T140s. The tub was riveted and bonded in L72 aluminium alloy and weighed only 70lb out of a total all-up weight of 1290lb – some 200lb less than the T142. The flywheel, starter motor and the adoption of a dry-sump lubrication system lowered the centre of gravity of the new car, and the Chevrolet V8 engine was fully supported in the chassis by extensions from the monocoque and a tubular spaceframe extending rearwards to a dural plate behind the gearbox. From this was mounted a novel type of rear suspension arrangement in which the normal lower link in tension joined the hub carrier between the outboard mounting points of a normal reversed wishbone. In addition to more positive longitudinal location, this arrangement permitted better alignment of the pivots of the various links to minimize camber and castor variations.

A Hewland DG300 gearbox was used in place of the LG600 as it was lighter and had a better shift. New driveshafts with Hookes joints to accommodate angular movement and a doughnut subjected only to plunge and torque loadings were used. The rear brakes – Girling ventilated discs of 12-inch diameter – were outboard of the carriers and deeply buried within the 17-inch-wide rims. Front suspension

Mario Andretti in the George Bignotti-entered Mark 3 which was powered by a four cam Ford engine. (Courtesy LAT)

was similar to the T142, by double tubular wishbones, but the steering rack now passed over the driver's feet.

The Lola-built Chevrolet 302 produced some 450bhp at 7500rpm with 48IDA Weber carburettors and Lucas or Bosch transistorised ignition. In testing, Mike Hailwood lapped Oulton Park at under the Formula One lap record of the day.

T190 development included wheelbase lengthening which eventually turned it into a Chevron beater, thanks to Frank Gardner. His T190X was a specially modified 1970 F5000 car; on the strength of such abilities Gardner became the Lola works development/test driver.

In 1970 Frank Gardner was third in the Guards European F5000 Championship, winning at both Thruxton and Silverstone in August. Mike Hailwood was fourth in the championship, also with two wins, despite quite a few spins. The results were: Gethin – eight wins, contributing

to a total of ninety points, Ganley – one win, lots of placings and sixty-one points (both drivers in McLarens); Gardner fifty-two, Hailwood fifty-one, etc. The T190 was only able to match or beat the McLaren M10B after Frank Gardner had developed it.

Jackie Epstein, who worked with Lola at the time, said: 'We [Epstein and Mike Hailwood] had done some pre-Christmas testing with the T190, and it was very good. Most people think that we fabricated the times Mike achieved at Oulton Park, but they were correct.

'The funny thing was that the testing was done on Goodyear G18s, and the G20s used in 1970 were worth another second a lap, yet we couldn't equal the test times until the second meeting at Oulton (the Gold Cup). The first car was the one sent to Sebring for Penske and Donohue, who found it basically good and competitive.

'Owing to understeer on the slow corners there was a geometrical design change at the front end and the jig

was altered; this made the car worse. Eric couldn't reproduce exactly the geometry of the original car and during 1970 we tried every conceivable type: we tried anti-dive, anti-squat, no dive, no squat, variations in between, heavy camber change rear links, nil camber change rear links, everything we could think of. In certain circumstances the car was very good – it was good on fast, open corners – but it was never predictable and the handling characteristics changed from circuit to circuit. This is what made it such a tough proposition to keep it competitive.

'In 1970 all our engines were built by Lola, who set up their own engine shop. This was an expensive exercise but was necessary because the American-built engines were never consistent enough. Alan Smith was already fully committed – and also we felt that Sid Taylor would get his best engines! We learned a lot about engines. The car was just too twitchy;

The Scooter Patrick/Ed Leslie Lola T70 Mark 3 GT coupé at the Sebring twelve-hours of 1968. The AIR, James Garner-entered car led, only to be put out of contention with steering problems. (Courtesy LAT)

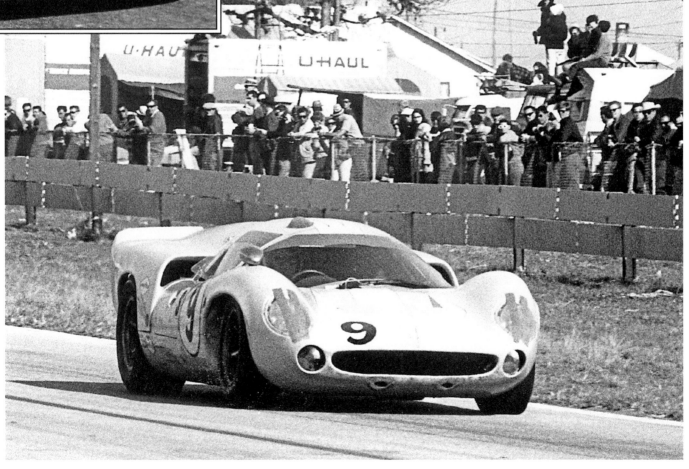

The first T70 Mark 3 coupé, SL73/101, at the Racing Car Show of 1967. Paul Hawkins stands at the extreme right.

it's notable that every T190 ever made has been crashed.'

In May 1971 Frank Gardner had overseen lengthening the wheelbase from 88 to 91 inches and later to 97 inches. The opportunity was also taken to widen the track and lower the nose. This was the Thruxton and Silverstone winning specification – and thereafter Frank was the man to beat.

The T192 made its debut in September 1970 with a 100-inch wheelbase. Gardner won from flag to flag at Warwick Farm in Tasmania in a T192 which sported an aerofoil just behind the front wheel. The T192 reached its full potential as a long-wheelbase T190.

En route to the Rothmans 5000 title in 1971, Frank Gardner won at Snetterton and Mondello Park (with Mike Walker in a T192 second) and at Castle Combe in his T192, and then drove to a second and two thirds before the car was replaced by the T242/300 in mid-season (after Gardner had realised the threat from Mike Hailwood's works Surtees TS8). Mike Walker scored a total of two seconds and three thirds in his T192.

Monoposto champion Chris Featherstone made his F5000 debut in the ex-Gardner/Guthrie T190/2 – otherwise known as the T190X – at Brands Hatch in September 1972, reappearing again in October.

Ian Ashley in a T190 took fastest F5000 lap in the Formula One Challenge at Brands Hatch in October 1972 in the original T190/1 (the 1970 model with a wheelbase of an extra three inches) despite the presence of newer models. The race was won by Jean-Pierre Beltoise in a BRM.

The price of the T190 was £8,300 complete, ex-works.

T70 – Mk 3 Spyders & Coupés – 1968 – 25 built

By the end of 1966 Lola had produced forty-seven T70s, and Eric Broadley now saw that he could produce a Group 6 coupé version for Endurance events in Europe.

Group 6 was the category coined by the CSI (Commission Sportive International) to cover so-called Sports 'prototypes'. This term described cars such as the Ferrari P-series and the Ford GT40 which were pure endurance racers (though Ford management did attempt to adapt their product for road use).

Furthermore, if the T70 Spyder production was taken into account, Lola would be able to homologate their new coupé into Group 4 when the required fifty examples had been completed. Broadley's interpretation of the rules led him to believe that this would happen and he therefore designed the Mark 3 which could be used in both Spyder (Group 9) and coupé versions (Group 4 and 6) simply by swapping bodywork.

Jackie Epstein found his experience with a T70 in 1966, when Paul Hawkins was driving his car in the first Can-Am events, meant that with the deletion of Group 7/9 racing he could use a Group 4 coupé based on Epstein had been racing a Ferrari 275LM in long-distance sportscar events until

Jo Bonnier's ex-Aston-Martin-engined SL73/101 at Oulton Park in 1968. (Courtesy LAT)

Paul Hawkins in Sl73/102 in the streaming rain at Spa-Francorchamps for the 1000km event in 1967, just ahead of Mairesse's works Ferrari P4. Hawkins gave the new coupé an excellent debut. (Author's collection)

outclassed by Ford GT40s, and now he approached Eric Broadley with the idea of assembling a coupé body on the T70 Spyder. Ideally he would also have liked a Ferrari V12 engine behind him, but Lola could see a bigger market by retaining the American V8 they had used previously.

It was at this time that Lola and Aston Martin arrived at an agreement in which the second Team Surtees Mark 2 was used as a test bed for Aston Martin's new five-litre V8 with which they intended to replace their trusty twin-camshaft six-cylinder engine in their road cars. They were pleased with the results, even though the engine put a connecting rod through the side of the block due to oil starvation while testing in the T70 Spyder.

The differences between a Lola T70 Mark 2 and 3 were few. The front and rear bulkheads were narrowed by two inches per side at the pick-up points for the suspension links, these being lengthened from 50 to 70 inches to give revised geometry. The top of the front uprights were machined slightly differently to suit the new set-up, while wheel widths were now up to eight inches front and ten inches rear (although still 15 inches in diameter). The track remained the same as a Mark 2. The steering rack was from a BMC 1800 instead of a BMC 1100, and knock-off hubs could be specified with beautiful polished cast-alloy three-eared spinners fitted.

Twelve-inch inch ventilated disc brakes with light-alloy four-pot calipers were fitted together with Lola-designed bridge pieces, and the twin-wishbone suspension had self-aligning roller bearings and ball joints. The first Chevrolet engines used in the new coupés were 5.5-litre Ryan Falconer tuned units with crossover inlet manifolds for the sidedraught Weber carburettors.

The racing tyres available were improving in leaps and bounds at this time with Firestone pioneering the flat crown type for Formula one in 1966. The T70 Mark 3 was designed around these tyres which called for the tread to be kept parallel to the surface of the road and suspension design now became more critical than ever before. Tread width was to grow steadily year after year from this point.

The car also featured an easily changeable radiator and oil cooler with an oil reservoir fitted at the front of the car, alongside the master cylinders in the case of the dry-sumped Aston Martin-engined cars. The dashboard assembly could also be changed quickly. It was not, however, a rapid job to convert the open car to its closed version and *vice versa*. A conversion kit to give the LG500 gearbox five speeds instead of four was offered in the USA.

Jim Clark, a New Zealander, had designed the sensational new coupé for Specialised Mouldings to make. It was

SL73/135, the road-going T70 Mark 3 coupé built by Franco Sbarro when shipped to Carl Haa's showroom in the 1970s. Note the central gearchange.

the first racing car to feature carbon-fibre reinforced bodywork. The beautiful bodywork had been designed – using a wind tunnel – not only with low drag in mind but also to give a measure of downforce front and rear. A notable feature were the gullwing doors fitted with a positive lock 'T' handle on the outside to try and overcome the problem of doors lifting at speed, which the Ford GT40 had suffered from. The side windows, made of perspex, had small diagonal flaps which could be fastened

in the open position to provide some cooling air for the driver. (The latches were parts from the Vauxhall Viva saloon.)

From the front of the car, the quick-release nose section had a wide grille opening to duct air into the front-mounted radiator which then exhausted through a slot in front of the windscreen. Large brake-cooling intakes flanked the grille opening, with single headlights mounted behind perspex covers above them. Mirrors to provide a vestige of rear view were usually fitted on top of the front wings, and small angled spoilers were sometimes added by race teams to their own designs. These were fitted

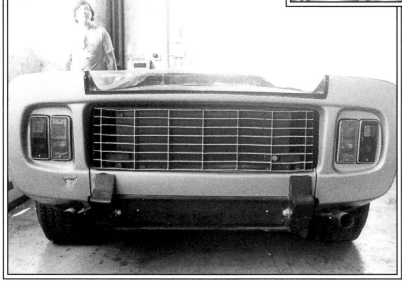

Bonnier again in Sl73/101, which he shared with Sten Axellson in the 1968 Sebring twelve-hours. Water in the fuel forced them to retire. (Courtesy LAT)

in between the brake-cooling ducts and the front wheelarch.

The windscreen was bonded into the bodyshell (rather than mounted in a rubber grommet) in the central bodywork section, which was attached to the monocoque by means of spire nuts. The front and rear body sections were quickly detachable with pippins. The rear body section featured cooling ducts on each side of the cockpit bulkhead plus two more small openings facing forward on the top of the rear deck which forced air into two aluminium 'periscope' type cooling ducts to the rear brakes. The mandatory spare wheel was mounted horizontally at the rear of the car, just inside the bodywork and above the gearbox. It was visible through the large cooling slot cut into the back.

Some customer cars, however, had their spare wheel fitted vertically.

To match the front spoiler bibs, trim tabs of aluminium, which could be adjusted for height with four bolts, were fitted across the top of the rear bodywork. (Some teams simply riveted them on in a fixed position). The twin exhausts exitted straight through the large slot in the centre of the rear bodywork and a 'luggage space' was mounted beneath the rear of the car. Full lighting equipment was carried in the coupé and one large single wiper blade was fitted to sweep the screen.

A full-length aluminium undertray was employed and ground clearance was set to four inches. In the monocoque itself, a stiffening rib was fitted in between the driver and passenger compartments while another ran in line

with the lower mountings for the front wishbones. The new dashboard was supported by an alloy box section which strenghened the tub at the juncture between the big sill compartment and the nose section.

Ron Bennett, having prepared a GT40 (1001) previously, commented on the reason a GT40 would ultimately go faster in top speed than a T70: 'If you look at a GT40 in plan view, it's a coke bottle in shape. Ultimately it passes through the air with less disturbance than a T70 coupé. We went around Silverstone with, I think, Laurie Bray driving the coupé with wool tufts all over it. It was doing around 60-80mph with cameras all around it and I asked Eric [Broadley] "What's it like?" and he answered, "I think we'll just race it as it is!" We cut away underneath

The aluminium spoiler on the John Surtees entered "Longtail" T70 Mark 3 coupé at Le Mans in 1967.

the nose because we always reckoned that was a high-pressure area, you could see all the oil from other cars collecting there.'

Production of the Spyder as a Group 7/9 sports racing car continued alongside that of the coupé, and in all a total of thirty-one Spyders and twelve coupés were built at Slough. The last Mark 3 in the shape of a rolling chassis was sent to Franco Sbarro in Switzerland. He fitted it out as a road-going car with air conditioning, electric windows, leather trim and silencing.

Lola themselves say that they did make one coupé as a road-going car, painted it silver and sent it to America to be displayed in a dealer's showroom. This car featured a ZF gearbox. Factory records have this down as SL73/117, a car later raced by James Garner's AIR team.

The first coupé, fitted with a Chevrolet engine, was displayed at the 1967 racing car show in British Racing Green with a white stripe painted longitudinally. Like the 1965 roadster and the Mark 6 before, it was the star of the show. This car had already been earmarked for team Surtees, another was on order, and both were destined to use the Aston Martin V8 engine.

The new, Tadek Marek-designed engine had the project number DP218. With wet cast-iron liners in its aluminium alloy crankcase, the 90-degree V8 featured chain-driven twin overhead camshafts, two valves per cylinder, and on a compression ratio of 11:1 with four Weber 48IDA carburettors gave 421bhp at 6500rpm and developed 386lb/ft of torque at

79

The four side-draught, twin-choke Weber 58mm carburettors fitted to Jackie Epstein's SL73/105 in 1967.

5000rpm in its first development stage.

These figures rose to 450bhp and 413lb/ft of torque in the engines which were slotted into SL73/101 and SL73/121 for the semi-works team which had been set up by John Surtees in conjunction with Eric Broadley. The prefix SL, incidentally, indicated that the car had been built in the new Slough factory as against the earlier set-up in Bromley.

It was as the factory geared up for its 1968 production run in late 1967 that a bombshell was delivered by the CSI, the governing body. They decreed that Group 4 cars would have to be made in batches of twenty-five and powered by five-litre engines as a maximum size in order to limit speed. The CSI had been concerned by the ever-increasing speeds of endurance racers such as the seven-litre Ford GT40, and this new ruling was a 'knee jerk' reaction to cars such as these.

This ruled out Lola's intention to

Jo Bonnier in Sl73/101 with a borrowed nose section, leads Mike D'udy in Sl73/105 on his way to second place in a GT event at Oulton Park in August 1968. (Courtesy LAT)

count in the previous Spyder production to qualify the T70 coupé for Group 4, and yet, ironically, it was to lead to the fastest sports prototypes ever seen, the Porsche 917 and the Ferrari 512.

T70 Mk 3B Coupé – 1969 – Group 4 – 16 built

With the Mark 3 coupé homologated into Group 4, Eric Broadley developed the Mark 3B coupé for the 1969 season. His reasons were simple: he now knew, having designed the T160, that he could raise the torsional stiffness of the monocoque tub, lighten the whole car and give better controlled suspension movement in a completely new package.

Although the car that resulted, the 3B coupé, looked similar to a Mark 3 (with the exception of the four headlight nose), under this beautiful skin all had changed.

The new all-alloy monocoque bore more resemblance to the T160, the 1968 works Can-Am car, than the old Mark 3. Bonded and riveted, it employed two detachable magnesium castings behind the cockpit area to assist in changing the engine and gearbox unit. Only the left-hand sill unit now contained the fuel, although some teams used a double filler system which was, for want of a better description, a 'bolt-on goody'. Thus, thirty-two gallons of fuel could be pumped into the engine via twin Bendix electrical pumps. Above these pumps, situated behind the cockpit unit on the left, was the oil cooler for the gearbox, while a similar cooler, mounted on the opposite side above the large oil tank for the dry-sump lubrication system, cooled the engine oil.

With torsional rigidity now up to 5000lb/ft per degree, this new T70 (or T76 as its drawings and chassis number prefix gave it) could now make use of the T142 running gear which it featured. (The T142 was the contemporary F5000 car). New cast magnesium uprights were held in Eric Broadley's twin-wishbone suspension system with self-aligning roller and ball joints at the front, while the rear suspenson employed a reversed bottom wishbone, top link and top and bottom radius rods, the bottom pair locating on the engine mountings. The steering rack was once again a BMC part from an 1100, but great care had been taken to ensure that bump steer could be adjusted minutely.

Brakes were radially ventilated 12-inch by 1.1-inch mounted on light alloy bells with four pot aluminium full-area long-distance pads fitted. The

SL73/121, the second team Surtees Lola Aston, outside his workshop at Slough in-between races in 1967. (Courtesy Lola Collection)

An extract from the publicity leaflet that accompanied the launch of the Mark 3 coupé.

LOLA TYPE 70 MK. III G.T.

SPECIFICATION

TRACK 58 inches

WHEEL-BASE 95 inches

GROUND CLEARANCE 4 inches with fuel and driver

CHASSIS Light alloy and sheet steel, monocoque construction

BODY Glass fibre

SEATS Formed in the structure and covered with lightweight quickly removable upholstery

FRONT SECTION Quickly removable for access to cooling system and front suspension

REAR SECTION Quickly removable for access to engine compartment and rear suspension

SUSPENSION Front Double wishbone on self-aligning roller bearings and ball joints. Telescopic shock absorbers and co-axial coil springs. Steering—rack and pinion.
          Rear Double wishbone and radius rod on self-aligning roller bearings and ball joints. Telescopic shock absorbers and co-axial coil springs.

BRAKES Girling disc. Front and Rear: 12¼ in.dia.disc. B.R. light alloy caliper. Vented discs optional extra.

WHEELS & TYRES 15 inch rim diameter, cast magnesium knock-on wheels.
          Front 8 inch rim width for 10.60 x 15 Firestone, 550 x 15 Dunlop or Goodyear equivalent.
          Rear 10 inch rim width for 1200 x 15 Firestone, 650 x 15 Dunlop or Goodyear equivalent.

ENGINE Chevrolet 333 cu. in. V8 standard. Ford or other V8 engines to special order.

WEIGHT Less driver and fuel 1760 lbs. With Ford 289 cu. in. engine 1660 lbs.

G.T. ENGINE SPECIFICATION

CHEVROLET V8

BORE 4.04 inches

STROKE 3.25 inches

CAPACITY 333 cu. in.—5.5 litres. 460 B.H.P. at 6,200 r.p.m.

Cast iron block with 4 bolt steel main bearing caps. Fully counter-balanced crankshaft. Light alloy flywheel and single plate diaphragm light alloy clutch. Special high duty connecting rods. Forged pistons. Cylinder heads ported, flowed and polished. Special valves, double valve springs and light alloy rockers on needle roller bearings. High lift race camshaft with roller followers. Four Weber 48 mm. downdraught carburettors on light alloy manifold. Special baffled wet sump lubrication. High capacity oil pump.

radiator was mounted at the front of the car, with the top canted forward, and an air box channelled the cooling air from the elongated slot in the nose section. Alongside this box on each side ran brake-cooling hoses which linked up to aluminium castings attached to the uprights to aid brake cooling. At the rear this air was ducted in through intakes in the top of the rear bodywork, allowing the air to pass down alloy 'periscopes' to the brake discs.

The bodywork was the first to make use of carbon fibre strengthening strips which were laid in a 'grid' fashion inside the nose and tail section, helping to keep them lighter and stronger than the Mark 3 units.

The rear bodywork was wider than a Mark 3, to accommodate ever-growing tyre widths, wheel widths being options of 8 or 10 inch at the front, 10, 14 or 17 inch at the rear. Track varied between 54 and 57 inches, depending on wheels and tyres fitted, but the wheelbase remained as a Mark 3 at 95 inches.

The doors were now hinged forward, for it was felt that this was safer for emergency driver exit; also to prevent a loss of the doors at speed – which had happened on occasion with the gull-wing type of the Mark 3.

The nose section was completely altered, being brought down much nearer to the ground to provide extra downforce. This gave the opportunity to add another pair of headlamps behind longer perspex covers. In effect, the bottom lip of the radiator intake now became a splitter, forcing air away from the flat underside of the car.

SL76/138, the ex-Redman, Hulme and Gardner Sid Taylor-entered car in later years when raced by Mike Wheatley. (Courtesy David Hodges).

At the rear, adjustable trim tabs were fitted to provide the same aerodynamic trimming as on the previous Mark 3 coupé. The cockpit section had the familiar bonded windscreen and a roll-hoop behind the driver's head. Weight was now down to 860kg, but the factory stated that re-homologation would be sought at 800kg. The standard engine offered was a Traco modified Chevrolet V8 of 304 cubic inches (five litres) breathing through four 48mm downdraught Weber carburettors, and the transmission was via the now usual Hewland LG600 five-speed and reverse gearbox fitted with 7¼ inch three-plate Borg and Beck Clutch. Large roller-spline driveshafts were employed to cope with the 480bhp the engine's builders claimed.

Twelve cars were laid down at the end of 1968; sixteen would eventually be delivered by the end of 1969.

SL76/139 was the first car actually delivered (to Roger Penske) on 30 December 1968, while SL76/138 was shown, painted in Sid Taylor's colours, at the 1969 Racing Car Show – where it drew unanimous approval.

T70 Mark 3Bs were raced by all the best 'privateers' in 1969-1970. The 1969 season started brilliantly with Roger Penske's car driven to victory at the Daytona 24-hour race. Alas, this car was later stolen, thus depriving Lola of perhaps the one team which could have achieved far more in international sportscar racing than all the other entrants. Nevertheless, when they were running well, they were always 'on the pace', even the Porsche 917 having to copy their bodywork style to succeed.

David Piper, that doyen of racing car drivers, bought a Mark 3B coupé, SL76/150, in 1969 and described it thus: 'The Lola T70 was such good value as a long-distance sports racing coupé at that time. It was a big step forward in all areas over the Ford GT40, against which it was measured. The car was comfortable and easy to drive with no vices at all – it was very forgiving in the handling department, the steering being so light: that was unheard of in a car with such huge rim widths, but of course Eric Broadley had been very clever in ensuring that the the main width of the wheels was inset, this no doubt contributing towards the feeling that so big a car could be made to feel so light.

'Of course the Achilles heel of the car was the iron heads on the Chevrolet engines; today that's all been cleared up, indeed the engine is now probably the most reliable part of the car! In summary: a cracking car, just terrific, and even today people remark on just what a beautiful car it is.'

Sid Taylor entered Lola T70s in both Spyder and coupé form for such luminaries as Denny Hulme, Brian Redman and Frank Gardner. He remembered the T70 well: 'One of the best cars ever made. Very simple and straightforward to run. It came out at the same time as the Lotus 40 and early McLarens and beat them easily. Of course McLaren got his act together in the Can-Am from 1967 on and beat the Lolas but till then … ! The coupés were beautiful too, just as easy and cheap to buy and maintain. We had the first car to lap Silverstone at 120mph and the first to lap Mallory Park at over 100mph. Great days.'

The Mark 3B sadly suffered its share of suspension breakages, but today it is *the* car to beat in historic racing – thus showing that if only (those magical motorsport words!) the teams had been blessed with more development money, the cars could have been so much more successful.

7
1970-1971

T200/202/204 – 1970/72 – FF – 120 built

The T200 series of Formula Ford racing cars was announced in November 1969 and was mainly intended for the USA, but Lola had hopes for European sales too. The T200 was built using a spaceframe with a Hewland Mark 8 gearbox.

This was Lola's first try at Formula Ford. Peter Hull and Tony Trimmer showed well in Europe; Mike Hiss and Ron Dykes did well in the USA in the inaugural year. Early in 1971, by finishing third to a pair of foreigners, Jody Scheckter won the RSA Driver to Europe Award in his Lola T200. *Autosport* stated that 'he is undoubtedly a driver with a great deal of talent and could go a long way.'

Wheelbase 88in
Front track 54in
Rear track.........................54in

T210/212 – 1970/71 – Gp 6 2-litre Sports – 38 built

The T210 series of sportscars was Lola's contribution to an era of great racing in Europe. Lola, Chevron and, later on, Toj all competed in a series of races which saw some very close racing. The T210 used an aluminium-skinned monocoque with a separate engine subframe, and the whole car was built to be as simple and uncomplicated as possible so that owner/drivers could maintain them easily. To achieve this the front suspension was the standard double-wishbone type and the rear the usual top link, reversed-bottom wishbone and forward locating radius arms.

Jo Bonnier was the European agent and his car was really a works effort, although it was race prepared in Switzerland. JoBo's 210 spent some considerable time being modified in Slough, the developments including magnesium uprights, new dampers and aerodynamic tweaks.

Racing in 1970

The prototype T210 was sorted out at Silverstone by Dickie Attwood in April 1970 for Bonnier, who was immediately the pace of the field against the Chevron B16 coupé. Lola had a weight advantage due to its Spyder form – the Bolton firm were caught on the hop and only really caught up when they introduced their open B19 Spyder version.

Nevertheless, the threat of the B16s *en masse* – together with a mystery brake fault seemingly inherent in his car – were enough almost to negate the sole effort of Bonnier, who just missed the title, having won four out of nine rounds (Salzburg/Anderstorp/Hockenheim/Enna) and placing second in two more. One of these was the nail-biting Spa-Francorchamps race where Brian Redman – enjoying an equally fantastic season with his Chevron B16 – just pipped JoBo at the last corner (La Source). Chevron thus beat Lola in the European Trophy for Makes by one point!

Autosport tested Terry Croker's T212 at Silverstone in their issue of 19 November 1970, and declared the success of the new FIA Two Litre Championship. Simon Taylor, then Editor, wrote: 'The Lola 210 is one of those racing cars which seem to

epitomise the attainable peak. It looks right, and it is right; in handling, braking, power, neat and superb construction it simply is *right*. When driving it, you experience that rare and indefinable feeling of being in command of a superbly efficient, complex piece of machinery which is doing exactly what is asked of it and is about as good as it can be, a device produced by a man to do a certain task as effectively as possible.' Taylor then sketched the background to the T210 before giving his driving impressions: 'Much of the car's speed comes from that fabulous little engine, with its instantaneous pickup the moment the throttle is touched: out of Becketts hairpin in second gear and up through the box to fifth, the acceleration actually felt much more impressive than the Formula 5000 car I had driven on the same circuit the week before, for the FVC seems to rev like an F3 unit. The gearchanges up the box follow one another so rapidly that it's best to steer with the left hand and leave the right hand on the gear lever. Woodcote demands a double gearchange from fifth to third, and then up to fourth

I tended to manage it better if I went from fifth to fourth, and then from fourth straight to second. Getting round Becketts is simply a matter of how neat and quick you can be, almost regardless of throttle opening or how early in the corner the power is turned on, for the Lola seems to be capable of taking full power in second round this hairpin without drama; it just stays glued down, handling neutrally, and rockets you off down the straight, although real hamfistedness will eventually make the car understeer and run wide.'

Taylor concluded: 'I'm smitten. My bank balance dictates that I can only love Lola from afar, that my infatuation for her will never be fulfilled. But smitten I remain.'

Most fast 210s used the Cosworth 1800cc FVC engine, and complete cars cost about £6000. Phil Scragg, the hillclimber with a penchant for hairy motorcars, having raced an E-type Jaguar and a Lola T70 with bodywork cut down so that it resembled a large Lotus 7, now ordered a Lola 210 to be fitted with a Ford 289cu in V8 engine.

Emerson Fittipaldi won the Brazil Cup sportscar series in a Lola T210 FVC from Jorge de Bagration's Porsche 908 by 30 points to 26, and Alex Soler-Roig was third with a 907 on 21. Wilson Fittipaldi was fourth on 15 points with a T70 Mark 3B coupé.

For 1971 Bonnier announced that his company was to do the preparation work on all four 'semi-works' Lolas for the year: two for Karl von Wendt's team (Helmut Marko plus rent-a-driver) and two for Scuderia Filipinetti (Elford and Bonnier). The cars were

past the pits; fourth gear is held until copse, so that at the braking point there one is almost at peak revs. A short, sharp stab on the brakes and a simultaneous downchange (when I managed the heel and toe right!) from fourth to third, and then the car is powered through copse.

'Back into fourth and fifth at the beginning of Maggotts, which even I was able to take flat; the car felt beautifully steady, and only the G-forces on one's body brought home that one was going round a corner at over 120mph. As a result the car was travelling at a pretty astonishing rate into Becketts, but so rapidly does it respond to the middle pedal that there is barely time to make three gearchanges to get to second gear by the time the braking is done, and

The same T212, twenty years later, at the "Trophee des Ardennes" at Spa-Francorchamps. The driver is Mauro Borella.

almost unchanged from 1970 – new rear uprights and relocated oil coolers being the major modifications although Bonnier also made some minor body and chassis changes.

Helmut Marko and Jean Pierre Jabouille won the first round of the European Championship at the Paul Ricard circuit in a T212 in April, followed by Elford, as Vic had slowed with electrical problems on the last lap. All this was achieved despite a spin by Marko. Nicki Lauda won for Chevron at the Salzburgring round two with Ronnie Peterson second for Lola at Silverstone in round three.

For the Targa Florio on 16 May Jo Bonnier and Richard Attwood placed third to the Alfa Romeo T33/3s of Vaccarella and Hezemens and de Adamich and van Lennep. Mixed in among a trio of 911Ss, Mike Parkes and Peter Westbury came fifth, and seventh was the Antonio Nicodemi/Jonathan Williams car. All these drivers were in T212s with Cosworth FVCs.

The only other FIA points earned for Lola that year were scored by Teddy Pilette and Taf Gosselin who came in sixth at the Spa Francorchamps 1000km the previous weekend in a T70 Mark 3B coupé (SL76/146) behind the Porsche 917Ks.

Just one week after sharing victory at the Le Mans 24-hour race with Gijs, Marko won the non-championship Auvergne Trophy at Clermont Ferrand, beating JoBo, with more T210/212s coming in 4th, 5th and 6th. Their win was aided by a new Firestone compound – but only after Larrousse's Matra 660 had sustained a puncture to finish third. Marko then swept Hockenheim in round four on 4 July, with Elford 2nd, to give Lola the lead in the championship – Bonnier only taking fourth – while Vic Elford debuted Bonnier's T222 into third in the Interserie event there. Guy Edwards won the non-championship Nogaro round in his T212 in August.

In a dramatic end to the season Vic Elford won at the Nürburgring round for the second consecutive year. But he was disqualified from third place in the next – penultimate – round at Vallelunga, having left the pits when the red light was on. Marko, who came in second, was thus the champion, as were Lola, despite Merzario winning for Abarth. Jo Bonnier won the last round, at Jarama in November, to make it Lola 57/63 points and Chevron 46/49 in the best eight scoring. Lola won five,

Lola T212, chassis number SL212/20, before running in the 1972 Targa Florio, in which it won the 1300cc class.
(Courtesy Mauro Borella)

Chevron three, Abarth one. Marko totalled 36 points and Elford 24. Antonio Zadra took third place at Jarama in a T210 behind Jose Juncadella in a Chevron B19.

Marko was absent from this round – as were many – and only thirteen cars took part. Instead, that same weekend, Marko was fifth (with John Love) in a T212 at the Rand 9 hours at Kyalami, where Terry Croker shunted Edwards' T212, making it the eighth chassis the team had destroyed that year! *Autosport* asked if the team was Lola's favourite customer! Marko and Love won round two at the Cape Town 3 hours with Edwards and Croker third in the new car behind Hailwood and Redman in a B19 with a Chevrolet Vega engine.

Helmuth Marko escaped unhurt from a crash at the next race, in Lourenco Marques, towards the end of the race, when he was in line to take the lead. He was classified fourth, and Chevron won. At the sixth and final round at Pietmaritzburg, John Love and Bill Gunston's T212 won from Guy Edwards and Jackie Pretorious (also T212-mounted) on 27 December. Jody Scheckter was third in a B19, thereby winning the Springbok title.

The Lola T212 and Chevron B19 were then made eligible for Group 5 when it amalgamated with Group 6 for 1972. The European Two Litre Sports Car Championship was to be for Group 7, the RAC Championship for both types. Surprising all, Gerard Larrousse won the first round of the European Two Litre Championship in an updated two-year-old T210.

Bonnier had beaten him into second in the first heat in a brand-new T290, but JoBo dropped to seventh overall with a pitstop for a loose cam cover in the second heat. Jean-Jacques Cochet was third and Edwards sixth, both in T290s. T210/212s were still very popular with privateers. Eric Broadley later said, in an interview in *Autosport*, that the T210 series became the basis of the T290 series.

T220/222 – 1970/71 – Gp 7 Can-Am – 9 built

Eric Broadley returned to the Can-Am series with the T220 in 1970, designing a simple and practical car for Peter Revson to drive under the Carl Haas banner. L and M cigarettes provided the sponsorship, and an aluminium big-blocked fuel-injected 8-litre Chaparral-Chevrolet provided the urge through the usual Hewland LG600 gearbox with fuel capacity of 68 gallons. The monocoque chassis followed the typical tried and trusted riveted and bonded aluminium format, and the suspension used a lot of components from the F5000 T190. The curvaceous body had been designed with as much downforce as possible; despite this, extra nosetabs still had to be added after the first shakedown runs. The brakes were by Girling.

In 1970 Peter Revson qualified fourth at the first race, Mosport, but he was still 1.8 seconds off Dan Gurney's pole in a McLaren M8D. In the race proper Revson retired with an oiling problem, but he had some good runs in the T220 (once second, twice third) and came in eighth in the final points to

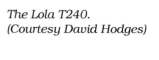
The Lola T240.
(Courtesy David Hodges)

Dave Causey's T163 – which was fourth – as the McLarens roared on. Halfway through the season Revson took delivery of a new T220, this one with a ten-inch longer wheelbase. Revson reported that braking stability was much improved!

In January, 1971 the T222 was shown at the Racing Car Show in London. With the longer wheelbase and wider track of the second T220, several examples were sold, some for the Can-Am and some for the Interseries. Vic Nelli bought one, as did Hiroshi Kazato who was just able to scrape into the top ten in 1971 in his T222 as the Lola team concentrated on the Jackie Stewart T260.

T230 – 1971 – F1 – Not built
T240/242 – 1971/72 – F2/FAt/FB
– 17 built

Of monocoque construction, the T240 was first seen at the Racing Car Show in January 1971. Helmuth Marko was to drive the semi-works Formula Two car, having done well in a T210 the previous year. His car was to be run by Karl von Wendt and Jo Bonnier.

Marko was eleventh in the first heat of the 1971 season-opener at Hockenheim, but he hit the barriers with an ill-handling car on lap four of the second part. The Lola was withdrawn from subsequent events while it was sorted out by Frank Gardner (and Marko). The T242 was an experimental 1971 F5000 car using a T240 tub, later renumbered T300. The T242 number was then reallocated for use on 1972 FAt/FB models.

T250/252 – 1971/72 – FSV
– 59 built

The Formula Super Vee T250, mainly designed by John Barnard, was first seen in January 1971 alongside the T240 and T222 at the Racing Car Show.

In 1971 Lola had to concede to Bill Scott in a Royale in the SCCA Super Vee series, with Tom Reddy and Tom Davey being the top men for Lola in second and third places, with a win apiece in the seven-race series. In 1972 Scott in the Royale did it again, the Lola T252 slipping back a place behind Harry Ingle driving a Zink, with Gregor Kronegard third.

By 1973 Lola was still sliding, coming fourth with Elliot Forbes Robinson in a T252 – who put in a late charge with two wins and then a second in the last three races. The series was actually won by Bertil Roos in a Tui. In 1974, using a T250-based Lynn and then a T320, Forbes-Robinson won seven out of the fourteen races (including the US Grand Prix support race) to take the SCCA crown by a wide margin from Harry Ingle in his Zink, runner-up for the third consecutive time.

In 1974 Freddie Kottulinsky won the first five of eight races in his ATS T252 and/or T320 to clinch the Formula Super Vee Gold Cup including the German Grand Prix supporting round. Keke Rosberg won at the Silverstone Tourist Trophy meeting in a Kaimann, while other contenders included the T320s of Helmut Bross and Prince Leopold

Von Bayern (Freddie's team mate) in a T252.

T260 – 1971 – Gp 7 Can-Am
– 2 built

The T260 was built in the new Huntingdon factory, with a very distinctive bluff, short nose. The monocoque used L72 and NS4 light alloys, bonded and riveted. There was capacity for sixty gallons of fuel in the sidetanks. Holes in the bonnet instead of a radiator grille admitted air to the coolant radiators. The front suspension was by unequal wishbones attached to virtually horizontal Bilstein spring/dampers units. At the rear were adjustable links with radius arms with a lower wishbone. Lola magnesium wheels were fitted as usual, and the brakes were outboard Girlings. The engine was quoted as 496 cubic inches – 8.1 litres – and 650bhp. Jackie Stewart was signed to drive in the Can-Am series, and the prototype was shaken down by Frank Gardner at Silverstone before leaving for the USA.

Jackie Stewart was on pole for his debut at Mosport on 13 June. He was out in front, but the gearbox ran dry, allowing the McLarens to sweep all top six places. He later won at St Jovite (passing a sick Hulme-driven M8 near the end, after hounding him all afternoon). Stewart then won at Mid-Ohio, where both McLarens broke and he soft-pedalled to victory by two laps on a crumbling surface over Seppi Siffert's Porsche 917PA ... but he was unable to stop the Supermacs who won all the other seven rounds. Fast yet fragile was the T260. Towards the

continued on page 113

The Coventry Climax V8 installation in the engine bay of BRGP 44, ex-Surtees, 1962 and Chris Amon, 1963. (Author's collection)

The Lola Mark 5. (Courtesy David Hodges)

*Left: 1968 Monaco Grand Prix
and John Surtees rounds Casino
Square in the T180/Honda.
(Courtesy David Hodges)*

Jonathan Williams in a T142 at Brands Hatch in April, 1969. (Courtesy David Hodges)

Left: Lola T142, Forbes driving, at Brands Hatch in the same race as Williams in April, 1969. (Courtesy David Hodges)

Right, main picture: T212 in the Karussel during the Nürburgring 1000km of 1970. (Courtesy David Hodges)

Right, inset: Brands Hatch, 1971, and Jo Bonnier climbs into his Scuderia Filipinetti T212 before the BOAC 1000km. (Courtesy David Cundy)

Above: Alan Rollison in a T300 in the Race of Champions at Brands Hatch in 1972. (Courtesy David Cundy)

Right: Guy Edwards and David Hobbs shared this Lola T290 in the BOAC 1000km at Brands Hatch in 1972. (Courtesy David Cundy)

Gijs van Lennep at Brands Hatch in 1973 in his T330. (Courtesy David Cundy)

Tom Belso at Brands Hatch in 1973 awaits the paddock marshal's call to take to the track. (Courtesy David Cundy)

John Foulston in the T260 at Brands Hatch with Chris Beauvoisin's T212 alongside. Sid Marlee, in a Chevron B19, completes the front row of the grid. (Courtesy David Cundy)

Inset: Teddy Pilette in a T400 during the Race of Champions at Brands Hatch in 1975. (Courtesy David Hodges)

Main picture: Lola Mark 1, David Pratley at the wheel in the FISA trophy race at Brands Hatch in 1989. Jeremy Agace in a Tojeiro Bristol follows on. (Courtesy David J Cundy)

Lella Lombardi waits to go out on to the Mallory Park track in her T300. Behind her is Teddy Pilette in the VDS-entered T330. (Courtesy David Hodges)

Tony Steele in his Mark 2 during the Formula Three historic race at Brands Hatch in 1990. (Courtesy David J Cundy)

Later years: SL160/9, the ex-Chuck Parsons car when owned by Rod Leach of Nostalgia *fame and used on the roads of Britain. (Courtesy Rod Leach)*

Graham Hill in the T370 during the 1974 Monaco Grand Prix.
(Courtesy David Hodges)

Stirling Moss pilots his own Lola Mark 1 at the Coy's festival in 1994. (Courtesy David J Cundy)

The T250 at the Racing Car Show of 1971. (Courtesy David Hodges)

end of the year the car was fitted with a bow aerofoil to increase downforce and cornering power. Stewart's car was sold at the end of the season to Jerry Hansen, and the unused spare went to the newly retired John Greenwood for Tony Adamowicz to drive.

Bob Nagel resurrected the T260 in 1973, finishing fifth in the points behind a quartet of 917/30s. The highlights of his season were a third at Mosport in round one and a fourth at the Riverside finale. Nagel gained four fourths in five races, and John Gunn (third at Elkhart Lake) was fourth and fifth the next year when Shadows ruled after the big guns pulled out with the glory days of the Can-Am all but over.

There would be a two-year gap until the series returned in 1977. Interviewed in *Autosport* Eric Broadley said the T260 was one of the first Lolas developed in the wind tunnel.

Overall length .... 139 inches
Overall width .... 76 inches
Wheelbase .... 98 inches

*The Formula Super Vee T250 of 1971
outside the works at Slough.
(Courtesy David Hodges)*

Front track .... 58 inches
Rear track.................... 58 inches

By the end of 1971 Lola had notched up sales of 135 cars during the year, totalling £500,000, and 90 per cent of their products had gone for export. Lola had been in their new, purpose-built factory in Huntingdon for a year, having left their scattered premises on the Slough Trading Estate in January 1971. The cars built at Slough had chassis number prefixes 'SL', whereas those built at Huntingdon would feature the prefix: 'HU'.

Peter Jackson's Specialised Mouldings had also moved to the Huntingdon Trading Estate, thus continuing the association which had prospered between the two companies. Their wind tunnel was of particular benefit to Eric Broadley's designs. Arch Motors, another Huntingdon company, was engaged in building the spaceframe chassis of the Super Vee and Formula Ford Lolas.

During the year Lola cars had won the Rothmans Formula 5000 Championship with driver Frank Gardner, the The European Two Litre Sportscar Championship and the Springbok series. Their agent in Europe was Jo Bonnier, and in America Carl Haas had taken over from John Mecom. Frank Gardner was the official test and development driver for the company, thus overcoming a lack of technical

Jackie Stewart in the Lola T260 during the CanAm season of 1970. (Courtesy David Hodges)

feedback which had previously been a problem, since they had now ceased to try and run a racing team, preferring to sell cars to customers instead. Mike Hailwood had been the previous test driver but had not been able to pass on to the designers the feedback they needed.

The Lola factory in 1977.
(Courtesy Alexandra Studio)

The ex-Stewart T260 at Brands Hatch in later years.
(Courtesy David Cundy)

8

1972-1973

T270 – 1972 – Indy – 5 built

Bob Marston and Patrick Head worked closely with Eric Broadley on a design, announced in April 1972. The first car went via Haas for Gene White and the second one probably went to STP. The chassis was a monocoque which stopped short aft of the cockpit with A-frames to carry the engine. The T270 was designed around the Ford turbocharged unit but it could be adapted for the Offenhauser engine. The bodywork featured a distinctive full-width nose, big side fences and side radiators as per the T260 Can-Am car. Lockheed brakes were in use, mounted outboard at the front and inboard at the rear, and a Hewland LG500 two-speed gearbox and roller splined driveshafts were used. The bag fuel tanks accommodated 75 US gallons of fuel, and the wheel sizes were 15in x 10in fronts and 15in x 14in rear. Wheelbase was 103½ inches while front and rear track was 61½ inches.

In 1972 Sam Sessions was fourth at the Indy 500 for Gene White Racing in a T270; Dick Simon was thirteenth in an 'old' T150-series and Wally Dallenbach came in fifteenth in the STP T270. Mark Donohue won for Penske/McLaren from the Parnellis of Al Unser and Joe Leonard. A real Lola 'Old Boys' day! No

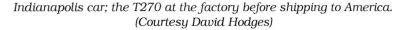

Indianapolis car; the T270 at the factory before shipping to America.
(Courtesy David Hodges)

The Scuderia Filipinetti Lola T282. (Courtesy David Hodges)

The T280 of Chris Craft and Gerard Larrouse during the BOAC 1000km at Brands Hatch in 1972. (Courtesy David Cundy)

more real Lolas were entered until Al's Haas/Hall T500 in 1978 ...

After the Indianapolis 500, Lloyd Ruby used a Gene White Racing T270 at Pocono and elsewhere that same summer, as did Wally Dallenbach.

T280/282/286 – 1972/77 – 3-litre Sports – 9 built

The T280 series of three-litre Sports-racing cars was the result of Jo Bonnier, Lola's European agent, exerting pressure on Eric Broadley. Bonnier had, he thought, secured sponsorship from Karl von Wendt's racing team, but when that worthy dropped out of the deal Bonnier was forced to take over the running of the two-car team and, with over £100,000, of his own money invested, Jo had to drop the talented Chris Craft from the driver line-up and take on Hughes de Fierlant who could pay for his drives.

The T280 was first tested at the Paul Ricard circuit, alongside the T290 by Derek Bell and Frank Gardner, in December 1971 – breaking the lap record – with a chassis similar to the T210. This was a monocoque with a rear engine subframe which could be changed to switch from three-litre to two-litre specification, all else staying the same. Featuring the well-known Cosworth DFV Formula One engine, the T280 was similar in looks to a T260 and was seen later on with side radiators and fully adjustable rear aerofoil. The T280 proved a fast car while it ran, but was too often let down by an inadequate budget.

Jo Bonnier and Reine Wisell shared chassis number two at the Buenos Aires World Sportscar Championship debut on 9 January 1972 (Gerard Larrousse and Chris Craft sharing the original number one). This was fifth on the grid, and Reine set the fastest race lap, finally coming in seventh. Wisell began half a lap down – after the car failed to start – but worked his way up to fourth inside twenty laps and was actually leading for a lap during the early pitstops. The T286 had climbed to third place by the second lot of stops, and at this point JoBo decided to put Larrousse aboard instead of himself to avoid any possible disqualification. (He had upset the organisers during an argument about Chris Craft being black-flagged.) Two laps were lost when Gerard Larrousse took over, then the gearbox eventually expired while the car was in third place (behind the two works Ferraris). Larrousse and Craft were seventh on the grid and did not finish. At the start they had swiftly climbed to fourth but slipped back to ninth with tyre problems. Chris Craft was black-flagged for leaving the pits on a red light, but after the car was pushed away it was reinstated! Making up time fast, the Craft/Bonnier/Wisell car eventually finished seventh, including a fastest lap 0.2 seconds faster than the Ferrari's pole! Bonnier's car was sold after the race to a Brazilian driver.

In Florida Jo Bonnier and Reine Wisell were fourth on the Daytona 24-hour grid behind a trio of Ferrari 312PB. The T280 of Craft/Larrousse/Nestor Garcia Veiga was seventh in practice but finally started following electrical problems (just like at Buenos Aires!). Wisell gradually worked his way through the field until he was right on Regazzoni's tail on the banking at 185mph – when the Ferrari had a rear puncture, its ripped bodywork smashing the T280's nose, damaging the windscreen and flattening the top of the steering wheel. More pieces hit Wisell's hand and helmet. Reine took the lead from the spinning Reggazoni, but held on for only yards, the Lola peeling off into the pits (where it lost six minutes). The Lola's instruments were out of order, but soon the car was back up to seventh, when the engine started

making funny noises. More stops, more delay and finally the DFV quit at about the ten-hour mark. The Ferrari lost fifteen minutes in the pits but still came fourth, and the other two Ferraris were first and second with the Alfa Romeos third, fourth and fifth.

The Lola was fastest on the Mulsanne straight in the Le Mans 24-hour race in testing, despite using an old type DFV engine, yet it was still eight seconds a lap off the Ferrari 312 times. JoBo and Hughes de Fierlandt easily won the poorly supported four-hour race by three laps from the Michel Dupont and and Jose Dolhem Chevron B19.

Bonnier, Wisell and Larrousse were then fifth at the Sebring twelve hours in the sole T280 despite umpteen component failures (exhaust, upright, radius arm ...) due to the bumpiness of the track. Once again the Ferrari won from Alfa. The Lolas were fifth and sixth on the BOAC grid at Brands Hatch, but both failed to finish after Wisell had led during the first pitstops.

On to Monza, but both Lolas were retired after sixteen out of seventy-four wet laps. Matters did improve at Spa, however, where Larrousse and de Fierlandt came fifth, although third was a Chevron B21 as a Ferrari One-two made it seven from seven. The T280s missed the Nürburgring 1000km and the Targa Florio in preparing for Le Mans, a reputed 48,000 man hours going into the preparation, with many modifications of Bonnier's own devising. Bonnier/Larrousse/van Lennep (standing in for an injured Wisell) were fifth on the Le Mans

24-hours grid with a second T280 for de Bagratron/de Fierlandt/Mario Cabral coming in ninth.

Using less revs (only 9400), Lola hoped the Cosworth DFVs would survive. Bonnier led lap three when one of the Matras was already out, but he was demoted by Francois Cevert two laps later. JoBo was ahead again on lap eight only to lose his position to de Fierlandt. In the wet, he pulled out half a minute on the field until the first pitstops when he dropped to fifth. De Fierlandt was third after four and a half hours but then the car lost time in the pits with front brake problems. Finally, that Lola was out around midnight when no clutch meant the car could not restart following an off into the Mulsanne sand.

Meanwhile, JoBo had all manner of early gearbox problems, dropping back. He was up to eighth by 8.00am but then collided with Florian Vetsch's Daytona while lapping it at Indianapolis corner and went off into the trees. Jo Bonnier, safety champion, died en route to hospital, leaving a wife and two children. The date was 11 June and Lola lost not only their European agent and a stalwart of the driving scene but a gentleman.

Gerard Larrousse and Vic Elford qualified second at the Österreichring but were out early with ignition problems and Ferrari made up the first four finishers. Finally, at Watkins Glen, the Wisell/Larrousse car qualified fifth but was out early after being hit by a Corvette. Ickx battled wheel to wheel to snatch victory in the final few laps from team-mate Peterson in yet

another Ferrari One-two. The season had promised much yet delivered little. It did, however, dispel the rumour that the DFV was not an endurance engine – it was probably the most reliable part of the mechanical equation!

The season actually ended with Larrousse and Beltoise winning the Paris 1000km at Rouen in October from pole with a fastest lap in the debuting T282. The new model was merely a cleaned and tidied version of T280. Second was the T290 Vega of Lafosse and Coulon one lap down. Oddly, very few of the T280 family were sold, the total supremacy of the Ferrari 312s deterring even the most ardent privateer – despite the Lola having set the fastest lap at Buenos Aires, in its first race.

For 1973 Gitanes and Antar were to sponsor the Filipinetti T282 in the World Sportscar Championship for Wisell (who turned down F1 chances in its favour) and Jean-Louis Lafosse, whose only previous experience in a three-litre was at Kyalami where he wrote off the Bonnier T280 after only two-and-a-half laps!

Joined by de Fierlandt for the debut at the Daytona 24 hours, the unsorted car qualified fourth but was out of the race at about midnight with electrical problems. The car was so new that there

The T286 outside the Lola factory before delivery to the Otford Group. (Author's collection)

wasn't even a spare engine. This was the year of the Peter Gregg and Hurley Haywood surprise win in a Porsche Carrera 911RSR.

Wisell and Lafosse came in a troubled sixth at Vallelunga in Round 2 (after being outqualified by the Barclays T292) as Matra held off three Ferrari 312PBs and the Jost/Casoni Porsche 908/3. They were sixth again at Dijon as Matra won at home from Ferrari. The Giorgio Pianta/Pino Pica T280 DFV was seventh and the Migault/Rouveyran T282 DFV retired.

A week after Reine won a wet Nürburgring Formula Two he missed the Spa 1000km to do more F2 at Pau, and so Lafosse was partnered in the Scuderia Filipinetti-entered car by De Fierlandt. Lafosse crashed; the wreck could not be repaired in time and was withdrawn as the the news came through that George Filipinetti had died of a heart attack.

The Lola T286 in the Otford Group's factory when raced by Jim Wallis (right) and Mike Wilds prior to the start of the season. (Courtesy David Hodges)

The only big Lola at the Nürburgring 1000km for Round 7 was Pianta's. Here Casoni replaced Pica but they did not finish.

There were two T282 models at the Le Mans 24 hours but neither finished, as Matra finally beat Ferrari. The T282 was not represented at the Osterreichring either in Round 9 (which was won by Matra) or at Watkins Glen. The Wisell/Lafosse car had been damaged at a Magny Cours test session the day before departure.

In the non-championship Imola 500km in September Mario Casoni was third, behind Bell in a Mirage and Stommelen in an Alfa Romeo T33, in an ex-Bonnier car now owned by his former chief mechanic Heini Mader.

T290/294/296 – 1972/81 – 2-litre Sports – 101+297/298/299 built

The T290 was first tested at Ricard alongside the T280 by Bell and Gardner in December 1971. It was to be fitted with a Chevrolet Vega engine (which had proved fast but unreliable in the recent Springbok events). Chassis number one was shown at the Paris Racing Car Show in January, 1972 and featured a Chevron-type shape with new suspension. Guy Edwards ran a works-blessed Barclays T290 (his need for about eight tubs the previous year had obviously worked!) and he did much of the development work. Guy won the RAC race on the car's debut at Snetterton on Good Friday from lots of Chevrons, leading throughout and with a record lap too. Then he won his class and was seventh overall (with David Hobbs) after Francois Migault and Barry Robinson's Chevron B21 was disqualified for being twenty kilos underweight. It should be noted that Guy used the Cosworth FVC for both successes.

The European season got off to an

ominous start when the new car was beaten by the updated T210 of Gerard Larrousse at Ricard in the season opener. Bonnier had beaten him into second in the first heat in a T290 but he had dropped to seventh overall with a pitstop for a loose cam cover in the second heat. Jean-Jacques Cochet was third and Guy Edwards sixth, both in T290s.

The Zadra and Pasolini T290 was fourth in the 1972 Targa Florio to take the two-litre class, and Edwards was second overall to Merzario in an Abarth at a wet Silverstone Martini Trophy. Swiss driver Claude Swietlick won Vila Real in Portugal in July 1972 from John Bridges' Chevron B21 and Carlos Gaspar's T280. Vic Elford had led in his T290 at one point. Jean-Louis Lafosse (in the second JoBo car) was the bright light in an otherwise gloomy season when he won the European Two-litre Sportscar Round 7 at the Nürburgring 500kms on aggregate for Filipinetti, as the faster runners flopped, and de Bagration was third. Lola led the championship with one race left. Alas, they were beaten; Jarama saw an aggregate win for Abarth, by Derek Bell, with Nanni Galli second and another Abarth sixth. In between came a trio of Chevron B21s. The best Lola could do was eleventh. Thus Merzario in the Abarth took the drivers' laurels, Abarth took the makes laurels with 112 points, Chevron 109, Lola 105.

Abarth entrant and engine supplier Enzo Osella had hedged his bets by mating one of his units to a Lola chassis in case the Abarth did not work, but this was not needed.

The Lola T292 made its debut with Richard Scott at the 1972 European Two Litre Sportscar finale at Jarama. It featured a wider track, revised bodywork and inboard rear brakes. Scott was second in the first heat, despite having a down-on-power engine, and he led the second heat until first he was spun out by Galli and then suffered vanishing oil pressure. Despite these vicissitudes he still came home in twelfth place. (The price for a T292 in the 1973 season was £4850 for a rolling chassis.)

Noritake Takahara and Tomohiko Tsutsumi were first and third in the Fuji Grand Prix in March 1973. This was the first of a five-race series. Guy Edwards was to run two works-backed Barclays T292s in the European Two Litre Sportscar Championship, for himself and SCCA man Jim Busby. This marked the return of the factory to the status of being a full entrant in a major championship.

Guy outqualified the Wisell/Lafosse T282 at Dijon in the World Sportscar Championship Round 3 but in the race the engine blew up. Then in the European Round 2, in Misano on 6 May, he won the first forty-lap heat and led the second … until his Chevy Vega block cracked four laps from the end, thus handing the heat and overall win to Chris Craft's T292. Guy was seventh. The T292 FVC of Santos and Mendoza was sixth in the Spa 1000km, while the T290 of Nicodemi and Moser was fifth at the Targa Florio to uphold Lola honour. Craft won the European Championship Round 3 at Imola in Martin Birrane's Crowne

Racing T292 BDG, but neither heat. Larrousse won the first heat in a T292 with a BMW engine but did not finish the second part. Lola now had 52 points, Chevron 50, March 28, Abarth 24. Then Edwards won Round 4 at Clermont Ferrand from series leader Craft. Called the 'Chris Amon of Two Litre', his luck finally held when that of others – notably Merzario in an Abarth and Larrousse driving a T292 with a BMW engine – ran out. Good fields, close racing, lotsa variety; a good series. Carlos Gaspar won the non-championship Vila Real 250km road race in his T292 FVC on 1 July 1973. He was the first Portuguese to win it for over twenty years.

At the Imola 500 in September, T292 number 62 appeared with a two-litre engine made by one Romeo Ferrari. A V8 made from two one-litre units with new block and crankcase, but with the same old pistons and heads, it was fitted to an ex-Bonnier car by its new owner Heini Mader. In the race it was driven by Giancarlo Gagliardi, who spun it around and did not do it justice. Ferrari's engine was subsequently seen in 1974 and in an Abarth at the Monza 1000km in April 1975. Duilio Truffo was the quickest two litre at Monza but the smart-looking engine (a new model?) had its troubles.

The 'Ferrari' engine was also seen at the 1975 Österreichring in a Lola T292 owned by Ferrari and driven by Manfred Mohr/Martino Finotto. It was much modified, including new crankshaft and oilways, and was to finish sixth overall, three laps down on the class-winning March.

Returning to 1973, Edwards won the Osterreichring race overall, being first in the opening heat and second in the later run, to close to within one point of Craft, who suffered engine problems early on. (Both had T292 BDGs.) John Burton was seven points ahead of Chris Craft with third in his Red Rose Chevron B23 FVC. At the final race, at Montjuich in October, Craft was on pole, with Edwards alongside and Larrousse and Burton immediately behind. Chris won the first heat from Gerard, reversing the order in the second part to give overall victory to the Frenchman's T292 BMW and the title to Craft. Guy Edwards and Richard Burton both had problems and so Lola won the title with 112 points to Chevron 92 and Abarth 76. Craft scored 70, Burton 62, Edwards 54. (Twenty-seven cars were sold in 1973.)

The T294 was a full monocoque with the engine and Hewland FG400 gearbox acting as stressed members. The suspension was by double wishbones at the front with a reverse A top link and twin radius rods at the rear while ventilated discs with Girling four pot calipers took care of the braking.

Front track 53ins
Rear track........................... 53ins

The T294 was quoted as:

Overall length 159ins
Overall width 73ins
Wheelbase 92¼ins
Front track 55ins
Rear track........................... 55ins

Rikki Von Opel had his first ever sportscar race in a T294BDG at the Nürburgring round of the Interseries. He was sixth in qualifying, but had a good run spoiled by an off-song engine

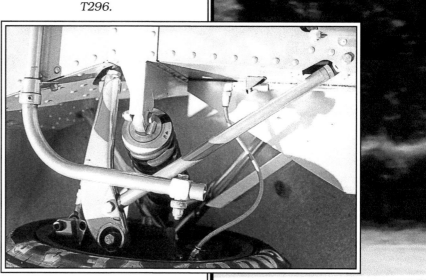

Front suspension detail of the T296.

– and retired from the race and racing. There was a T292/4 at the Le Mans 24 hours for Fred Stadler and Co with a Hans Funda-built two-litre Chrysler Simca engine from which 290bhp was claimed. When Funda died at the end of the year Stadler kept the project going. Entered by ROC, it was fastest qualifier in its class, but the electrics failed on Sunday. Later the Lola was fifth at the Misano Two-Litre round.

The Chrysler Simca engine was also seen later in some Chevron F2s, and it would win the two-litre class at the 1978 Le Mans race ... so the work was not in vain. The ex-Craft T292 made its debut at Misano driven by Jassaud and featuring a Tecno F8 engine. The Lola qualified third but its race was a catalogue of woe. A T292

T296 at Le Mans in 1978.
(Courtesy David Hodges)

Inset: Rear suspension detail of the T296. (Author's collection)

The ex-Edwards Lola T296 in America, 1996. (Author's collection)

with a BMW engine won the Nova Lisboa Six Hours in July in Angola – despite a bridge collapsing onto the track at the start! The car was driven by local men Antonio Peixinho and de Albequerque. An 'ex-Hailwood/Ickx Gulf' GT40 was sixth, driven by Emilio Marta, one place adrift of a Mini-Cooper S. Tony Birchenough and Roger Heavens won the second race – the Benguela 500 – in an ex-Edwards/Barclays T290, the only outright Dorset Racing win to date. The third race at Luanda won by a March 74S.

In 1975, Ian Harrower and Claude Crespin were eighth overall and class winners at the Enna WSCC in May, driving Birchenough's Lloyds T290 (now updated to T294 spec., excluding the outboard front brakes).

Crespin and Ian Bracey were eighth at the Österreichring 1000km in the Dorset Racing T290-4. Other T292/T294s included the ROC T294, still with a Chrysler Simca engine (seventh at the Hockenheim round of the European Two Litre Sportscar Championship

with Reudi Jauslin fifth in a T293), and Martin Raymond's, until he switched to a Chevron.

In 1976 Helmut Bross came a terrific third among a host of Porsches in the opening round of the World Sportscar Championship at the Nürburgring 300km in a T292 BMW two litre, having qualified fifth ahead of the new Edwards March 76S three litre. The pair of Dorset Racing T290-4FVCs of Birchenough/Bracey and Harrower/Richard Down did not feature, and DRA's ex-Edwards car was now in full T294 spec. The second car was also an updated ex-Edwards T290, albeit with the old-type bluff nose for better straightline speed and stability. Even so, Porsche won all eight races, including the non-championship Le Mans 24-hours.

Helmut Bross later won the two-litre class in the Kassel-Calden round of the Interseries and then the Mainz-Finthen round in October. He also scored a third and two runner-up finishes. Charly Schirmer also won an

Interseries two-litre round, at Zolder in May, with a third and fourth too. Ian Harrower and Simon Phillips were ninth at WSCC Monza Round 2 in their T290-4, behind the Morand/Trisconi T292. Tony Birchenough and Ian Bracey were sixth at Imola WSCC Round 3 as the Martini Porsches won again. This car was now designated by *Autosport* as a T294S FVC. (Confused you will be!)

Mike Hall was seventh at the Mosport 200 in T294, second in class to Tony Cicale's Chevron. The race itself was won by Jackie Oliver's 8.1-litre Shadow DN4. Herbert Muller joined DRA for the Dijon race, getting both cars onto the grid and upsetting some non-qualifiers. Brian Joscelyne, Ian Bracey and Herbert Muller finished eighth, second in class to the Lafosse/Jaussaud Chevron/ROC Chrysler, after Guy Edwards and John Lepp crashed with broken suspension only ten laps from the end.

In 1977 Alain de Cadenet and Ernst Berg were third at the Dijon round of the WSCC in a DRA T294S as

Alfas began their steamroller assault on the 1977 Group 6. Berg and Simon Phillips were then seventh at Monza as Osella tried holding onto their fellow Italians ... Lola were third in the championship while Harrower/Berg and Martin Birrane were unclassified at Le Mans after myriad problems. At least they got there, however, as they did not complete the seventy per cent of the distance required. The other DRA car was, apparently, the previous year's de Cadenet, but it did not qualify following a lot of lost practice time with a dry session engine change under the ACO's 'nationalistic' interpretation of the qualification rules. Guy Edwards then bought the Ultramar/Rizla T296 with a Cosworth BDX for the 1977 World Sportscar Championship. Chris Craft was an excellent fourth driving it at Estoril behind trio of Alfa T33s, winning the two-litre class, and DRA cars were third and fourth in their class of five starters and four finishers.

Ray Mallock then drove the T296 at Paul Ricard for Round 6 and was into third place before gear linkage and fuel metering problems stopped him. The top Lola was thus the T296BDG of Georges Morand and Christian Blanc with Frederic Alliot. Guy Edwards and Ray Mallock were fourth with it at the Salzburg finale, also behind three Alfas, but they did win their class and so Lola (on 55 points) were third in the makes' championship behind Alfa on a perfect 160 and Osella, 73. Lola did beat Chevron on 48 (which did not score in the last race.)

In the 1977 Interseries, Helmut Bross had the overall lead after 4 of 6 rounds by virtue of excellent two-litre results in his T294BMW. Jorg Obermoser in the TOJ (Modus) chased him. For the 1977 Can-Am, Bobby Rahal was a stunning sixth overall, being quickest at the Mosport Can-Am round in his T296BDX, but Mike Hall in a T294BDG won the class after Bobby's gear linkage went awry. Even so, Rahal was a good sixth at the finish of the Trois Rivieres race.

Price when new: £4850 (rolling chassis).

T300 – 1972 – FA/F555 – 15 built

Frank Gardner had originally seen the possibility of slotting a Chevrolet 5-litre V8 engine into the Formula Two car, the T250. This car had a reputation for difficult handling but the installation, with appropriate strengthening, of the heavier engine cured all of that; indeed, the T300 series were known as good-handling cars. The T300 was notable for its high side radiators and the now ubiquitous aluminium monocoque with the engine being used as a semi-stressed member. The front suspension used double wishbones with steeply raked back, almost radius rod type rear arms at the top, and outboard coil spring/damper units. The rear had transverse top links with radius arms and wide-based bottom links with diagonal bracing. Brakes were Girling 10.5-inch ventilated discs, outboard at the front, inboard at the rear. A five-speed Hewland DG300 gearbox was in use behind the ubiquitous Chevy 305-cu in V8 engine. Steering was by rack and pinion and the fuel tank capacity was 30 US gallons. Wheels were split rim with cast magnesium centres and were 11 inches wide at the front and 16 inches wide at the rear.

The model made its debut at Thruxton for Round 10 late in July 1971. Gardner finished third overall after two fifteen-lap heats. Frank qualified in pole position – after the car had been built in only three weeks! The new car was second next time out, at Silverstone. It was now called the T300 and featured modified front pick-up points and F1-type airscoops above the carburettors. Third time lucky, Gardner won the F5000 class of the Oulton Park Gold Cup on 21 August, finishing third overall to Surtees (TS9) and Ganley (P153) on the aggregate of two twenty-lap heats.

Having qualified on pole and battling for the lead, the T300 began its fourth outing well but ended in a mangled mess when Frank tangled with Brian Redman in a McLaren M18 at Snetterton. Its replacement – the first production T300 – won the Hockenheim F5000 round in which Emerson Fittipaldi drove the turbine-powered Lotus 56B to be a runner-up, some 5.2 seconds back. Frank Gardner won both heats. The new T300 had taken just eight days to build before it was shipped to Germany. The title was clinched at Oulton Park next time out (with two rounds still to go), Gardner beating Mike Hailwood in a TS8 by 2.5 seconds in a straight fight . The T300 took pole and led flag-to-flag – and so Gardner was champion with 90 points, Hailwood/TS8 next up with 58, Mike Walker/T192 was third on 40, A.Rollinson/TS8 fourth with 35.

Frank Gardner takes the works-entered T300 to victory at Brands Hatch in October, 1970. (Courtesy David Hodges)

Frank Gardner was then 39 years old, possibly not the fastest but certainly the most consistent. He had started sixteen out of seventeen rounds, finishing fourteen. Hailwood failed to start five times, mainly due to engine problems. By this time, Lola had taken sizeable orders for the T300. The first car had been written off at Snetterton and the replacement built to win the title; Sandy Shepard then had the third car made, Graeme Lawrence the fourth, with others ordered by customers in New Zealand and America.

In 1972, Gardner won the Tasman opener at Pukekohe and the New Zealand Grand Prix from Hailwood's TS8 – just like old times! Hobbs was third in Kirk F White's McLaren M22. Graeme Lawrence was badly injured on his T300 debut run, after a crash while lapping the Stanton Porsche which

killed its driver, former saloon champion Bryan Faloon. The Lola cartwheeled and disintegrated, catching fire. Gardner had to give best to Graham McRae for the rest of the series and ultimately finished 2.7 seconds adrift at Sandown Park – whereupon he announced his single-seater retirement, saying he was getting too old and cautious!

Gary Campbell used an ex-Gardner T300 for the Adelaide finale, finishing seventh, while Hailwood's second to Hobbs/M18 pipped Frank for the runner-up position. So, McRae had 39 points, Mike 28 and Frank 25. Rollinson was to have a works-supported Duckhams T300 for Alan McKechnie in Europe (especially in lieu of Frank's retirement), while in America reigning US F5000 champion David Hobbs was to have a Hogan T300 alongside Brett Lunger. Hobbs won the second round

at Edmonton but was out of luck thereafter despite winning the first heat at Donnybrooke in mid-season. Eppie Weitzes capitalised on David's problems there, winning outright, with Hansen in a T300 second.

Thereafter Lunger won at Road Atlanta and Lime Rock, beating Brian Redman in a Chevron B24 both times, and took third in the championship, the unlucky Hobbs only an unreflective eighth.

Others campaigning T300s in 1972 included Bob Muir and John Gunn, while in Europe Rollinson won the Brands Hatch RoC category, tenth overall, having finished second to Redman in an M10B in the previous afternoon's 'warmer' (when McRae was disqualified for passing Redman under yellow flags). Allan was also victor in Round 2 at Mallory Park the following

T300, chassis number HU300/10, in later years. (Author's collection)

weekend and won a Brands Hatch clubbie single-seater race at the end of June, using it as a glorified test session.

Next month he won at Phoenix Park (third in heat one, first in heat two) in another F2/F Atlantic type field, plus Wattie in the Eifelland 721. Then in September he won easily at Brands Hatch to keep his championship hopes alive. He was second to McRae at Oulton in the penultimate round, with Gijs only fourth, and so Allan was still in with a chance at the double-points Brands Hatch decider ... but it was not to be: van Lennep's fourth was better than his own fifth place, as Gardner took third in a new T330.

In summary, the season was spoiled by niggling problems which could not be overcome despite help from Frank Gardner in testing. 'Down under', Ken Bartlett in a T300 won the Adelaide F5000 but came second to Frank Matich in a Matich A50 Repco in the Gold Star series, 36 points to 24. *(See Appendix)*

T310 – 1972 – Gp 7 Can-Am – 2 built

In July 1972 the T310, the new Can-Am contender, was announced and was shipped to America for Round 2 of the Can-Am series at Road Atlanta where the car was to be entered by Carl Haas in conjunction with Steed. The T310 was claimed by Lola to have the best downthrust-to-drag coefficient of any car in racing, and with its low shovel nose it was the longest and widest and flattest Lola yet – far removed from the T260 of the year before. The bodywork was developed in the wind tunnel of Specialised Mouldings. The rear wing was installed very low in order to create the minimal drag, and the twin radiators were in the sides, fed by air scoops set into the top of the bodywork alongside the cockpit.

Lola claimed that they had carried out a large amount of background work on the 310 which was built in 'about a week'! (*Autosport*). The T310 had a full monocoque with outboard front and inboard rear brakes while the previous year's T222 running gear was used for most of the car. Wheel rim widths were eleven inches at the front and seventeen inches at the rear. The dry-sumped big block Chevrolet to be used was to be built by Folz and was to be of between 8.2 and 8.8 litres. The T310 was tested by Gardner at Silverstone and Snetterton, and it was then sent on to Haas in America.

The T310's wheelbase was 105 inches – the longest ever seen in

Portrait of an F-5000 Car

Lola T-300

CHASSIS:
Aluminum alloy monocoque, using engine as a semi-braced member

ENGINE:
Chevrolet V-8, 305 cu. in. (5000cc)

GEARBOX:
Hewland D.G. 300, 5-speed, non-syncro, limited slip differential

SUSPENSION:
(Front) — Double A-arms; outboard shock absorbers with co-axial coil springs, and anti-roll bar;

(Rear) — Wide base bottom links with diagonal bracing, fully adjustable; transverse top links with radius arms, anti-roll bar and outboard coil spring/shock absorber units

BRAKES:
Girling 10.5" diameter ventilated discs, outboard at front, inboard rear

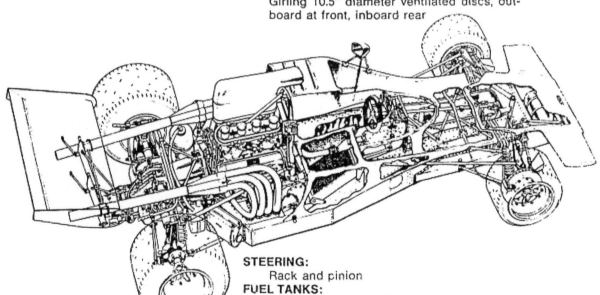

STEERING:
Rack and pinion

FUEL TANKS:
Safety rubberized fabric cells in monocoque; capacity 30 U.S. gallons

WHEELS:
Split rim, cast magnesium; 11" wide front. 16" wide rear

DIMENSIONS:
101" wheelbase, 58" front track, 58" rear track, 138" overall length, 35" to top of roll bar; weight, 1360 lbs.

the Can-Am series. Front and rear track was 66 inches and the weight was stated to be 1550 pounds.

At the car's Road Atlanta debut the T310 started eighth and finished seventh after overheating problems. Charlie Kemp was fifth in a T222. The T310's best result was a fourth place at Watkins Glen the next time out. David Hobbs finished up seventh in the championship, as the turbocharged Porsche 917 now dominated the series and Jerry Hansen purchased the T310 at the season's end. The T310 was the last Lola to be built for the great Can-Am series.

For one round of the European equivalent of the Can-Am, the Interseries, Herbert Muller was entered in a T310 fitted with a Morand-tuned 8.1-litre Chevrolet, but he did not start the event. In 1976 Bruce Langson came eighth in a World Sportscar race held at Mosport, a two-hundred-mile sprint in the 8-litre Lola T310. Alas, he received no mention other than in the result sheet!

T320/322/324/T326/T328 – 1973/77 – FSV – 92 built

Twenty-three T320s were built. The remainder were derivatives for the popular Super Vee Formula.

The T320 was campaigned in 1973 SCCA by the like of Wink Bancroft who scored two seconds en route to finishing fifth in the title chase.

Lynn used a T250 and then a T320 to win seven out of fourteen 1974 races to take the SCCA FSV crown.

Howdy Holmes and Freddy Kottulinsky campaigned T322s with increasingly good effect, Howdy finishing third in the seasonal finale at Daytona which Freddie won.

Freddie Kottulinsky won the first five of eight races in his ATS T252 and/or T320 to clinch the 1974 FSV Gold Cup including the the German Grand Prix supporting round. Keke Rosberg won the Silverstone round in a Kaimann while other contenders included the T320 of Helmut Bross and Prince Leopold Von Bayern (Freddie's team mate) in a T252. Freddie won the Daytona FSV in November in a Lola, presumably a T320.

American FSV Gold Cup visited Sebring for the first time in 1975 in the S12 Support. Bill O'Connor was on pole in new Haas T324 alongside Howdy Holmes, who led all the way (with best lap) in another T324. O'Connor was second. Eddie Miller won Road Atlanta FSV, the first FSV race for the former FF champion, his first time in a T324. Miller next won at Riverside for Haas with Howdy Holmes in a T322 coming second, Richard Melville in a T324 third and Peter Moodie in a T324 fourth.

Following a gap where SCCA files show he won at Lime Rock, Miller was eighth at Watkins Glen and then first again at Road America. He also won Round 9, the 'Canadian GP' at Mosport in September, his fifth success, beating Bobby Rahal in a Royale. Melville, Holmes and Alsup were next, all in T324s. Miller was second at Watkins Glen in October, to local expert Tom Bagley in a Zink by 2/1000ths of a second, but he clinched the FSV title with Daytona to spare.

Bobby Rahal in the Royale was third

and Keke Rosberg, on a debut run in a Supernova, was sixth behind the Lolas of Howdy Holmes and Bobby Lazier. The Daytona showdown with the top-line ATS team from Germany sank when the race was won by the almost unknown Herm Johnson in his T324. Bagley in a Zink was second, Holmes in a T324 third. Mikko in a T324 was only fourth.

Mikko Kozarowitzky in the ATS T324 won the 1975 Nürburgring Round 6 of the Castrol FSV Trophy after Rosberg/Kaimann blew up on the first lap. Lolas were also used by H.Bross and Manfred Trint. Keke still led the championship. Mikko won the next time too, at Diepholz, beating Rosberg by 0.7 seconds. Manfred Schurti then won the next round at the Nürburgring German GP Supporter with Mikko Kozarowitsky coming second, both in ATS Lolas. Eje Elgh was third. Kennerth Persson in a Kaimann was fourth to lead the championship. Rosberg in his Kaimann won the Silverstone F2 Supporter from Elgh and Mikko K's Lolas.

Kennerth Persson and Eje Elgh had won heats. McKechnie planned to test Keke in Richard Scott's Durex T400 at the end of the season. Mikko won at Zolder and looked good for the championship, although Elgh in a Lola was second. Kozarowitsky (Finnish and a former tennis pro) clinched the title with second place to team mate Manfred Trint (who spun early on but rejoined) at the final round at Hockenheim at the end of September. Elgh was on pole again but missed out in a typical slipstreamer. He finished fourth. Mikko Kozarowitsky was on 112 points, Persson 79, Elgh 66, Rosberg 52, etc.

Bagley in his Zink beat Herm Johnson in a T324 at Daytona FSV early in 1976 for a swift revenge (see above) for last year's finale. Friz Gleason came third and Benny Scott was fourth, both in Lolas.

Later, Bob Lazier won at Watkins Glen in his Tivoli Lodge T324, his first win of the year. Bagley in the Zink was second, Mosport was round winner and Bill Henderson was third in a T320. The star was George Follmer in his nephew's T324, setting the fastest lap. Lazier then doubled up to win Mid-Ohio from Bagley, driving a Zink, and Johnson in a T324. Bagley won the penultimate event at Elkhart Lake with the Lolas of Lazier second, Mike Yoder in a T326 third and Herm Johnson, again in a T326, fourth.

Brett Lunger made his debut in Formula Super Vee in a Lola on the front row, but he went out with engine problems when fourth on lap two. Bagley in the Zink also won the finale at the Watkins Glen USGP Supporter, taking the title; Johnson was second, William Henderson third, and Lazier fourth, all in T324s. So Bagley finished on 135 points, Lazier 123, Johnson 88, and Henderson 77.

John Morrison – long-time formula stalwart – won the British 1976 Formula Super Vee title in a T326. His wins included Mallory Park in July and Thruxton in August.

In mainland Europe Lola owners could not repeat the success of 1975 in 1976 despite the various efforts of Morrison, Axel Plankenhorn, Eje Elgh, etc. The Castrol and Gold Cup championships went to Mika Arpiainen in a Veemax Mark 8.

Oulton Park, Easter 1977, and a T332 works hard. (Courtesy David Hodges)

Arie Luyendyk won the 1977 Donington European F3 Supporter in his Rotel Hi-Fi TT28. Next were Daniel Herregods and Kees Trouw also in T328s. Axel Plankenhorn T326-8 had looked set for victory until his car's throttle spindle broke. Two days later Arie won again, at the Silverstone British F3 Supporter on Bank Holiday Monday, with Axel second after leading in the Warsteiner-sponsored car, Herregods and Trouw following on again. Luyendyk also won the Silverstone Tourist Trophy Supporter from a pair of Veemaxes. Plankenhorn had led again but spun off – as did Jag in the feature event! Jo Gartner was fifth for Kaimann. Luyendyk clinched the championship at Hockenheim in October with a second-place finish to Plankenhorn's third.

In America in 1977 Bob Lazier took the title from Herm Johnson, both in T324s. Lazier won six out of ten rounds, Lola eight out of ten with Herm Johnson and Stuart Moore (fourth) one each. Bagley in the Zink formed the only major opposition, coming third with two wins.

Price when new: £2180 (rolling chassis).

T330/332/332C – 1972/77 – F5000 – 56 built

The most obvious difference from the T300 was that, whereas the earlier car had a pontoon engine bay, the T330 had the engine as a stressed member. The rear wing was bigger too, in USAC style.

The T330 had a threequarter-length aluminium alloy monocoque. The front suspension used double wishbones while the rear had transverse top links and lower wishbones with radius rods. Lockheed ventilated discs were fitted, outboard at front and inboard at the rear. Gearbox was the Hewland DG300 and engine the Chevy V8, plus others. The T330 became a good and staple money-spinner for Lola with the T300/330/332/333 range.

Fifteen cars were sold in the first year of production, the T330 being debuted by an unretiring Frank Gardner at Brands Hatch in the F5000 finale in

October, the car not having been tested before first practice. The T330 qualified second and finished third behind the battling Redman and McRae, and this helped Frank Gardner clinch the Tarmac British Champion title from Roger Williamson.

Overall length	190ins
Overall width	81ins
Wheelbase	102ins
Front track	64ins
Rear track	64ins

Frank Gardner in the T330 F5000 Lola. (Courtesy David Hodges)

Mario Andretti in the Vel's Parnelli T332 in which he achieved many victories.

Price for the T330 for the 1973 season was £5650 for a rolling chassis. Twenty-one had been ordered by Christmas 1972, seventeen for the USA including one for Roger Penske's AMX effort. Four stayed in the UK, one for Guy Edwards, another for Ian Ashley, two for Jackie Epstein.

There were no wins at all in Tasman races in 1973.

In January 1973 it was announced that Radio Luxembourg was to sponsor two T330s for the defending champion Gijs van Lennep and Tom Belso (plus Gij's 1972 championship-winning Surtees TS11 for Carlos Santo – though he and Tom would be seen to swap cars later on). Haas was to run a pair of T330s for Brian Redman and Reine Wisell, overseen by former BRP man Jim Chapman. All four had works support but nothing was seen of Reine...

The Haggar Slacks T330s of Lunger and Hobbs were second and fifth respectively at the Brands Hatch season opener in the Race of Champions on the Saturday and Van Lennep was sixth for Radio Luxembourg in a weekend dominated by Chevrons, notably the winner Peter Gethin who took his B24 to a famous Race of Champions win next the day.

Peter Gethin was well out of it at Mallory in Round 2, when David Hobbs was the best Lola driver in tenth place, but the marque was back on form at the Silverstone International Trophy Support a fortnight later when Hobbs won from Brett Lunger. Gijs van Lennep then took a snowy F5000 class win and seventh overall in a Formula One race won by Jackie Stewart from Ronnie Peterson.

Brett Lunger then switched cars to give Trojan their first-ever Formula 5000 win, beating Van Lennep in a tense see-saw battle at Snetterton in Round 4

In Round 15 Ian Ashley won his first F5000 race when Hardwick in the Henley Forklift T330 won at the Jyllandsring in September, confirming his recent speed. It was the first win for the T330 in Europe in nine races and five-and-a-half months. In the final race of the year, Guy Edwards won his first F5000 victory at Zandvoort, by less than a length from an inspired Tony Dean in a Chevron B24, after John Watson had crashed his Trojan when clear of the field. Ian Ashley also crashed out on lap two. At the next race, at home at Snetterton, Bob Evans won for Trojan with Teddy Pilette in second place to keep the championship lead. The best Lola finish was Belso in fifth place.

Guy Edwards won the double-points finale at Brands Hatch after the epic dice of Watson and Holland in T101s and Ian Ashley in a T330. He used new compound Goodyears – untested – to great advantage, breaking the lap record too. Clay Reggazoni was twelfth and Teddy Pilette was out of luck but won the Championship with 136 points, Tony Dean coming in second with 133, Holland 116, Thompson 114 – and Guy Edwards scored 102 as the top Lola driver.

Shell Luxembourg (helped by the Surtees team) won the Teams' prize with 206 points to Dean's AAR 196 and VDS 160. It had been the best year for the formula to date, twenty-six F5000

Lolas being sold during the year. The *Autosport* season review later said that it was thirty-one. Whatever – not at all bad when Lola did not estimate making more than twelve!

In America in 1973, the Penske AMC-engined car was destroyed in a garage fire, and so the team missed the early L&M Championship rounds. Brian Redman won the Riverside Round 1 on the 29 April – in a conventional Haas/Hall T330, featuring deep JPS-type rear wing dams and a tall airbox – from Jody Scheckter in a Trojan and Tony Adamowicz in a T330. Hobbs with Gethin in his Chevron B24 came in fifth and Brett Lunger – in yet another T330 – sixth. Brian had decided against the twitchier car with its very modified suspension.

Mark Donohue's AMC-powered Sunoco T330 was third to Scheckter in the Trojan and Redman's T330 at their Mid-Ohio debut on 7 June. Jody's third consecutive victory was by 0.7 of a second; Tony Adamowicz was fourth. Scheckter's fourth consecutive win was a bit different, being at Watkins Glen in a Sid Taylor T330 after his Trojan was damaged in Friday testing. In a dozen laps Jody beat the record by three seconds, qualifying two seconds clear of the rest of the field. He won his heat and led the final from flag to flag, with a record lap to boot. Lola filled the top six places via Redman, Lunger, Donohue, Weitzes and Hobbs.

Brian Redman finally broke Scheckter's run, beating his Trojan by 2.5 seconds at Elkhart Lake in a thriller of a race, with Weitzes in a T330 third. Brian then won again at

Road Atlanta from Mark Donohue in a revamped T330 AMC, with Peter Gethin's Chevron B24 third and Jody Scheckter fourth in his back-up Trojan (having previously declared it his intention to race his very new T330). David Hobbs and Brett Lunger had yet more problems ... and then Brian won again, at the penultimate Pocono round on 3 September. However, Jody clinched the title with third place behind Lunger.

All the main protagonists of the year were in T330s. Brian Redman used the more modified of his two Haas/Hall cars; next up were Tony Adamowicz, Weitzes, Donohue and Hobbs for a T330 top six sweep. Brian then finished off the season by winning Seattle, with Donohue in his T330/AMC second (again), Scheckter third in a T101 and Tony Settember fourth in a M10B. Clay Regazzoni was there in the highly modified ex-Muir T330 of Chuck Jones and Jerry Eisert. He was third in qualifying and second to Redman in his heat, but he failed to finish in the final due to fuel feed problems. The car had been totally rebuilt since Muir's Road Atlanta shunt and featured a full-width front wing and distinctive rear one as well. Later on it was used at the Brands Hatch finale but came in only twelfth with handling problems and more fuel-feed dramas. Later Brian Redman announced he was to continue with Haas and Hall in 1974. Following his Can-Am successes Donohue announced his retirement.

Johnnie Walker won the 1974 Tasman opener at Levin in a T330

Repco, but Lola had to wait until Max Stewart won at Teretonga Park for their next T330 victory. Stewart then won at Oran Park from Walker with Warwick Brown, also T330 mounted, third. Chevron came back to win the next two races, and although Brown (still recovering from a monster accident the previous year) then won the final race, in Adelaide, Gethin, (in the Chevron B24) came in second and that was enough to clinch the title. Peter had 41 points, Stewart – who retired with a broken oil pump after leading – got 26, Pilette 22 ... etc. Max Stewart won the first round of the Gold Star at Oran Park in a T330 in August. Brown was second and Lawrence third, both in T332s. Stewart then won the second and third rounds at Surfers Paradise and Calder too.

In 1974 Ian Ashley and Lella Lombardi, for the Shellsport Lux team, used updated T332s and Guy Edwards was to run with Embassy sponsorship in his John Butterworth T332, as with Graham Hill in Formula 1. He wrote off one car at Silverstone the week before the first race at the Brands Hatch Race of Champions meeting. The T332 specification owed much of its redesign to Redman's Hall car of the previous year. Peter Gethin carried on where he left off in the 1974 Tasman series, winning Rothmans Round 1 at Brands Hatch Race of Champions meeting in the new Chevron B28. The next day, however, he was unable to repeat his last year's win, settling for third in class behind F5000 winner Ian Ashley's T330 and Steve Thompson's B24.

David Hobbs won the wet Mallory Park Round 2 in a Hogan T330, with Mike Wilds/Dempster's March 74A second, as in the Brands Hatch round. Guy Edwards had his third car in only two weeks – shades of early sportscar days! Brian Redman won Round 3 at Silverstone and won again at Oulton for Round 4, beating David Hobbs by 0.2 seconds. Minor placings went to Ian Ashley, David Magee, Lella Lombardi and Brian Evans for an all-Lola top six.

The Lola brigade were unable to reproduce this result at Brands Hatch two days later on Easter Monday, only getting the first three courtesy of Evans, Redman and Ashley. The duel between leader Evans and a fast-closing Brian Redman had been titanic, and Brian Redman had set a new outright lap record at 1 minute 43.8 seconds at 101.92mph.

Derek Bell, sitting in for Indy-bound Hobbs, led the Thruxton Round 7 from pole position in Hogan's T330 before dropping to fourth with a deflating tyre. The race itself was won by Ian Ashley in the Henley Forklift T330. David Hobbs returned immediately after the Mid-Ohio win to do so again at a very wet Mugello round, an event which only lasted a total of eleven laps. Bob Evans was second in a T332.

In mid-July Bob won the Mallory Park Round 11 by 0.2 seconds from Peter Gethin in another close encounter of the F5000 kind. Evans then took the Dublin Grand Prix at Mondello on aggregate from Vern Schuppan's Sid Taylor T332, having shared one heat win and a second place each. Bob made it a hat-trick at Thruxton, from

Gethin in his Chevron B28 and Belso in his T330. Schuppan had been the comfortable leader until his car's oil pressure went. Vern led the next race at Brands Hatch but crashed in the rain, and the race was then stopped. At the restart, on a drying track, Tony Dean's tyres held up better than those of poleman Evans – who was also pipped by Magee in a B24 – and so a third place kept the championship lead.

Five laps to go, and a puncture robbed Evans in the Oulton Park Gold Cup, dropping him to sixth and splitting the championship wide open. Ian Ashley took the biggest possible advantage to win in the Shellsport Lux T330. Next up was Snetterton, where the race was stopped after six laps due to rain, the order being Holland/Evans/Belso. After the restart, Thompson won the 'other' twenty-four lapper, and was given the laurels – which were then taken back when the stewards decided to add both parts together! When this was done the race went to Tom Belso in a T330 from Brian Robinson's M19C, Brian McGuire in a T332, with Thompson, Evans and Holland eighth, ninth and tenth respectively.

One week later Guy Edwards in the Embassy T332 had a great come-back race to win at Mallory Park (where he had broken his wrist three months before), leading for all but the first mile, which went to poleman Ashley before he spun down to twelfth. In an inspired recovery, he eventually came second, only two seconds adrift with a new lap record. Gethin was third, Lombardi fourth and Evans fifth. Guy Edwards was still in pain – but happy!

Vern Schuppan in a Chevron B24 won the finale at Brands Hatch in October by one second from Ashley (again). Gethin was third from front row but well out of contention with handling problems. Evans had been alongside on pole but his Chevy broke after four laps leaving him to bite his nails for forty-five minutes. It was his first non-finish of the season. Evans was the champion with 193/198 points (he would later win the top Grovewood award too); Gethin 186; Ashley 152; Pilette 108; Lombardi 88/89. The best fourteen out of seventeen rounds counted; however, Rothmans quit as the series sponsors after Brands Hatch.

Keke Rosberg drove the McKechnie/Henley Forklift championship winning T332 in post season testing at Silverstone. Rosberg was very impressive, despite having not driven anything more powerful than Formula Super Vee before. The winning car (with spares, engines, trailer, etc) was sold to Brian Maguire in January 1975, but in November Chevron had announced that they were quitting F5000 as they found it uneconomic (despite having new a design ready).

The 1974 Mid-Ohio Round 1 of the American championship saw Mario Andretti's VPJ Viceroy T332 (managed by ex-Haas and Lola Cars man Jim Chapman) hold off Brian Redman for half the race. After that Andretti's engine went off and he retired. Brett Lunger was second in his Eagle to the Lancastrian. At Round 2 in Mosport Andretti again led, only to fall back to fourth with more engine problems. Hobbs was the fortunate recipient of first place this time in Ted Hogan's T332, with Eppie Weitzes T332 second and Brett Lunger third in an Eagle.

Third time lucky, Mario, won the Watkins Glen Round 3 from the T332's of Redman, Weitzes and McRae – who had the pleasure of beating Sam Posey's Talon. (Talons were renamed GM2s, Graham having left the team after a recent argument.) As always Andretti was the only front-runner on Firestones. Brian Redman, incidentally, had a new Lola to replace his Mosport write-off.

Johnny Rutherford had his first single-seater road race in a Hogan T332 but hit the kerb and crashed after six laps, breaking his ankle. ('Lola ankle' was an acknowledged affliction!)

Round 4 was held at Road America. Mario won again, just holding off a late Redman charge as his engine spluttered with fuel starvation; Weitzes was third, then Hobbs and Tuck Thomas, all in T332s. With five weeks to the next race, Andretti and Redman both had fifty points.

At the first big race at Ontario in four years, since the Questor Grand Prix, Lola took all top seven slots. Redman won from Mario, who came through from the back of the grid, with a troubled Hobbs third. Then it was Mike Mosley, John Gunn, Jerry Grant and Tony Settember, all in T332s. Johnny Rutherford was ninth between two Talons in a roadcourse comeback. James Hunt made his F5000 debut in the new T332 of Ferrari dealer Francisco Mir, but although good in practice he had engine problems and failed to finish.

Brian Redman took the Laguna Seca win after leader Andretti suffered an exploding tyre, to finish third. Second was James Hunt in a new Eagle. Al Unser in a Chuck Jones T332 would probably have been fourth in the first non-USAC single-seater race had his engine not expired after twenty laps. Mario Andretti got his revenge at the Riverside finale, beating Brian by five seconds with Brown third and Al Unser fourth. Bobby Unser had won the second heat in a USAC Eagle Offy and led the final, only to drop a valve. James Hunt in the Eagle crashed, taking the impressive Vern Schuppan in a T332 with him.

Graeme Lawrence won the 1975 Tasman opener, the New Zealand Grand Prix at Levin, in a T332 by beating William Brown in a T332 by thirty-two seconds. Brown won a wet Pukekohe, and McRae in a GM2 then won Round 3 and Chris Amon in the Talon Round 4. Brown won Round 5 at Oran Park, leading the whole way from Lawrence and Walker, all in T332s.

Walker got top place in Round 6 at Surfers Paradise to take the championship lead, and Ken Smith was second in the ex-Haas/Hall/Redman T332. Adelaide, Round 7, ended with Lawrence, Brown, Walker and Amon in the Talon, with Stewart (fifth) and Bartlett (dnf) reverting to the older model after a very disappointing time with new Lola T400s. The first three were equal on points – with one race to go and all to race for! Brown clinched the title at Sandown Park in Round 8 with a solitary point for sixth, neither of the other two getting that far! The race was won by John Goss in a Matich from J McCormick in an Elfin and then the golden oldies of Stewart and Bartlett and Amon's Talon. Walker crashed out from pole position, Lawrence having had electrical problems. Brown had led from the start until two laps from home when he had to stop for fuel. He was the first local-boy Tasman champion in eleven years.

Later in the year, for the Gold Star series, McCormick, John Goss and Bruce Allison each won races, while the F500 T330 cars soldiered on in many races – drivers such as Walker, Stewart, and Allison all going well.

Things were better for the T330/332 in the USA in 1975. The season opener at Pocono was rescheduled by a month due to rain. In the meantime Hall and Haas had decided to forgo the new T400 and use the T332 which had been shunted by Mickey Rupp at Ontario the previous year. This used altered suspension, modified nose and oil radiators relocated from the sidepods to the rear, as in the T400. Owing to a changed model of car, the T332 had started the heat from the rear. It won this, and went on to beat the Viceroy T332 of Al Unser in the final. Mario Andretti had been up at the front until his engine (inevitably) blew.

Sticking with the T332s – as the chassis of the new models was still proving difficult to balance – Andretti won Round 2 at Mosport by 0.6 of a second from the ever-present Redman. (Brian had been forced to take a practice off when he had been clipped by the errant Don Furey in the ex-Donohue

T330AMC.) Redman won Watkins Glen Round 3 from Al Unser, both using 'old' T332s as did third-placed B J 'Bernie' Swanson. Jackie Oliver in the Shadow DN6 had led the first fifteen laps before his engine's head gasket blew. Mario Andretti in a T332 won a heat (as did Brian) but was only sixth in the final after a delayed start with fuel-flow problems. He did, however, set a new lap record. Andretti took Elkhart Lake Round 4 in a T332. Brian Redman retired from his heat (won by Oliver) when a rear upright broke, so he started the final in nineteenth place. He was up to second with a record lap when delayed by tyre and gearbox problems, and he had to be content with eighth at the finish. Eppie Weitzes was third in a T400 with modified T332 bits and which was referred to as a T432! Swanson was fourth and Elliot Forbes Robinson third on his F5000 debut in Evil Knievel's Mir T332, with 'Big Al' Unser sixth. Mid-Ohio Round 5 in August saw another Redman win but only after Mario Andretti had gearbox problems ten laps from the end, after Brian had hounded him all the way. Al Unser was second for Viceroy with David Hobbs third, also in a T332. He passed Oliver within the last six laps, having started at the back after engine problems when leading the heat. Swanson in a T332 was involved in a big shunt when his throttle stuck open at the start, hitting the armco barrier inside the track at the pits end, just before the bridge at first turn. He died three days later. A week later Donohue died of injuries received in Austria in a Formula One practice accident.

Road Atlanta was the venue for Round 6, Al Unser passing his Viceroy team mate Mario Andretti and then out-fumbling Redman to win by one length. He was the first new winner for a long time and the first by a USAC Oval hero in F5000. All three were using T332s. Jackie Oliver in the DN6 Dodge was fourth as the only non-Lola in all ten finishers! Round 7 was the inaugural race at Long Beach, won by Brian Redman to retain his SCCA/USAC title. The star was Tony Brise in a Theodore-entered T332 who, after winning his heat, got past the Viceroy Lola of Mario and Al to lead, spun, then forged his way ahead again. Unser clipped the wall trying to keep up and did not finish. Andretti's gearbox then went, and he was forced out. Then a halfshaft went on Tony Brise on lap thirty-five, and Redman was handed victory. Vern Schuppan was second in an Eagle, Weitzes third in a T400 and Chris Amon fourth in a Talon. Tony Pryce debuted well but failed to finish after problems with the gearbox and valves. Brian Redman commented that he was lucky to inherit the lead. Most spectators voted it the best F5000 race ever.

The penultimate Round 8 at Laguna Seca was a VPJ/Viceroy T332 benefit. Mario Andretti and Unser took the heats and then romped to an easy win, Mario ahead by two seconds at the finish. Brian Redman finished third in a rebuilt car after a crash in practice, and Tony Brise was fourth, both also in T332s. The race was a classic demonstration with lots of top finishers (unlike the European equivalent).

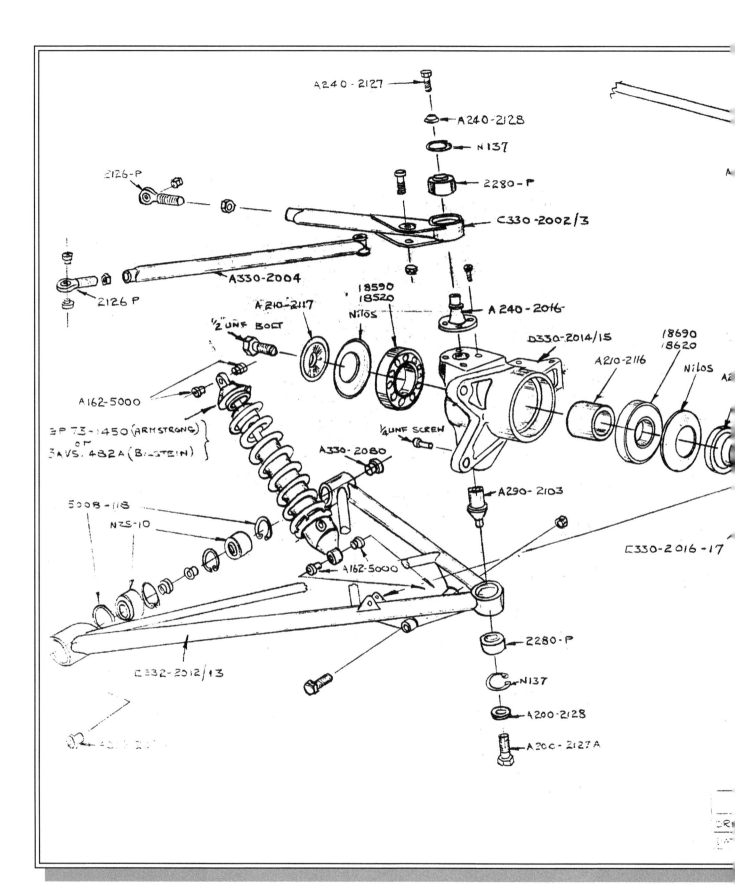

A240-2127

A240-2128

N137

2280-P

2126-P

C330-2002/3

A330-2004

2126 P

18590
18520
Nilos

A240-2016

A210-2117

½ UNF BOLT

D330-2014/15

18690
18620
Nilos

A210-2116

A162-5000

¼ UNF SCREW

3P 73-1450 (ARMSTRONG)
or
3AVS.482A (BILSTEIN)

A330-2080

A290-2103

5008-118

NZS-10

A162-5000

C330-2016-17

C332-2012/13

2280-P

N137

A200-2128

A200-2127A

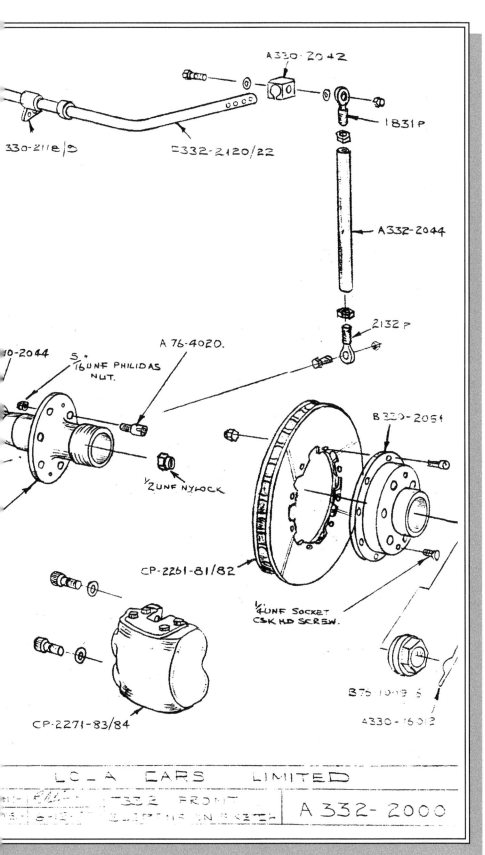

Original factory exploded view drawing of the T332's front suspension.

A330·2042

1831P

330-211e/2

=332·2120/22

A332-2044

2132P

0-2044

5/16UNF PHILIDAS NUT.

A76-4020.

1/2UNF NYLOCK

B330-2051

CP-2261-81/82

1/4UNF SOCKET CSK HD SCREW.

CP·2271-83/84

B76·1009·5

A330·16012

LOLA CARS LIMITED

T332 FRONT

| A332-2000

The final race at Riverside seemed rather familiar, Mario leading Al home again with Brian third – this time in a T400 as he had damaged his T332 in practice at turn nine. Tony Brise had been third and finished sixth after running dry on the penultimate lap. Viceroy pulled out of racing two days later. Brian Redman won the championship with 227 points; Andretti scored 165; Unser 161; Oliver 77; Weitzes 60; Hobbs 50; Brown 42; Schuppan 39; Swanson 32; Brise 17.

For 1976 this was not now a real Tasman – that had stopped in 1975 – but a series of races in New Zealand and Australia. Ken Smith, the new NZ Gold Star holder, won the New Zealand Grand Prix in January in an ex-Redman T332 at Pukekohe, and M Stewart won a wet Manfeild in a T400 from Redman and Allison. Smith then won at the Lady Wigram circuit at Christchurch, and although the T332 of Graham Lawrence took the final event at Teretonga one week later Smith was second to total twenty-four points. Allison was the runner-up, being fourth in both the last two races.

Vern Schuppan in the Theodore T332 won the Aussie opener at Oran Park and then finished second to Ken Smith at Adelaide in Round 2 when an almost certain victory for David Purley in the Oaten Lec T330 was snatched away after he collided with a backmarker after driving superbly up through the field from a humble start. John Cannon was the surprise winner of Sandown in a March 751 Chevy, née 73A. Schuppan was second and J Goss in a Matich third. It was the first win

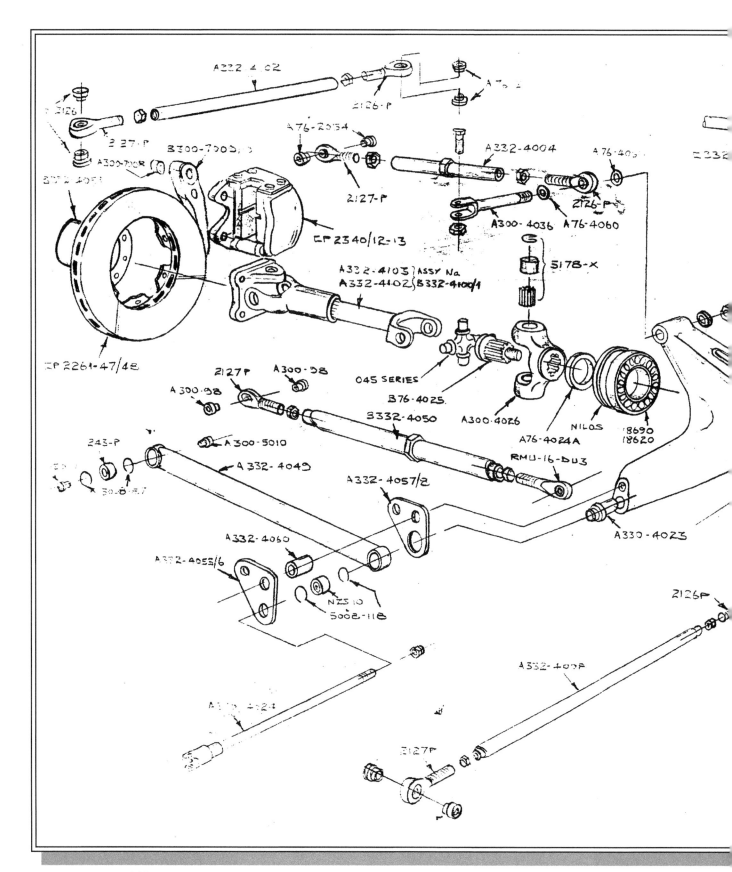

A222.4.02

2126

2126-P

227-P

B300-700S/6

A300-700R

A76-2054

2127-P

A332-4004

A76-40

2126-P

A300-4036

A76-4060

EP2340/12-13

A332-4103)ASSY No
A332-4102)B332-4100/1

5178-X

A332-4053

EP2261-47/48

2127P

A300-98

A300-98

A300-5010

A332-4049

045 SERIES

B76-4025

A300-4026

NILOS

A76-4024A

8690
18620

RMD-16-DU3

3332-4050

A332-4057/2

A330-4023

243-P

30-8-R.7

A332-4060

A332-4055/6

NZ510

5008-118

2126P

A332-409P

A332-4024

2127P

2127P

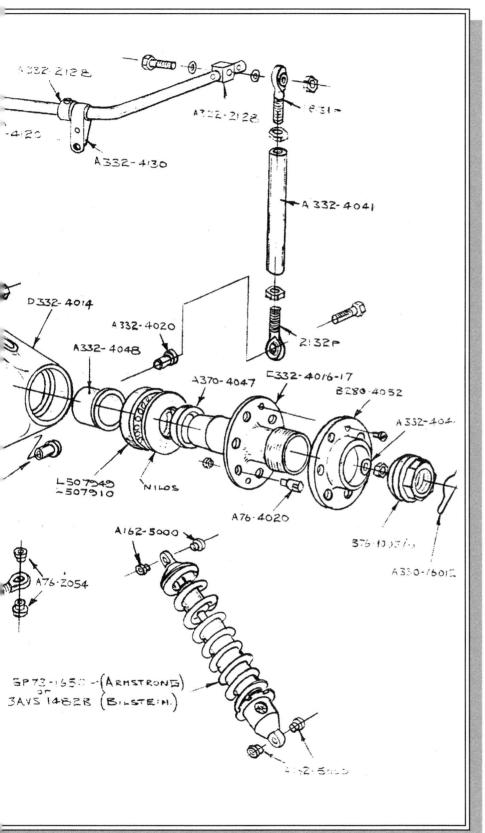

A332-2128

A332-2128

18-31

A332-4130

-4120

A332-4041

2132P

D332-4014

A332-4020

A332-4048

A370-4047

E332-4016-17

B280-4052

A332-404

A76-4020

L507949
-507910

NILOS

A162-5000

A76-2054

376-10.03/3

A330-76012

GP73-1650 - (ARMSTRONG)
or
3AVS 1482B (BILSTEIN)

A162-5000

for the Canadian since taking the 1970 USA series with Hogan's M10B.

Surfers Paradise was washed out, so Vern Schuppan was the Aussie champion and Smith the unofficial 'Tasman' victor of the combined totals of both series. At the end of the year Smith won the opening round of the New Zealand Gold Star, at Manfeild in October in his T332 from the similar car of Graham Lawrence, the only other F5000 car there. Formula Pacific was taking over. Smith also won at Raupuna Park, and Lawrence was again second in Round 2.

In Europe the 1976 T332C was unveiled in February with Pilette giving it a Silverstone shakedown. The small T332C featured a full-width nose and front radiators. Lola insisted it was a development car for two-, three- or five-litre engines and it featured a similar specification to the previous year's American F5000 winner for Brian Redman.

Alan Jones won at the Brands Hatch Round 4 on Easter Monday in Sid Taylor's ex-Belso T330 with pole position and a record lap, winning from flag to flag.

Brian Redman in a T332C won the 1976 season opener in America for the fourth consecutive time, but was behind Danny Ongais in an Interscope T332C for twenty-two laps until he spun down to second following a closely fought race. Teddy Pilette came in twelfth with the new T430 after experiencing problems. Alan Jones won at Mosport in a Theodore T332 from Jackie Oliver in a Shadow DN6B and Pilette in the T430. The Shadow had led until five laps from the end, when 'Ollie' made a slight mistake when being harried by Jones. Brian Redman had been thereabouts too, but fixing a stuck throttle dropped him to eighth.

At the next race – a wet Watkins Glen – Jones again snatched the win in the last few laps but this time aboard a March Chevy 76A. He had been forced onto the grass (with Redman) when Al Unser spun at the first corner in his first F5000 outing of the season – from pole! The (temporary) leaders Pilette (in the T432) and Brown (in a T330) spun away their advantage so that Oliver led inside two laps despite starting on the eighth row! Then it was Jackie's turn to spin, in the process splitting the sump and throwing away a one-minute advantage. Brown led again, only to be passed by a recovered Unser, but now Jones – who had replaced a chunking tyre – was fastest by far. He took over at the front, two laps from home ... phew! It had been the first non-Lola victory since June 1973! Lola had all nine other finishers though, consolation places going to Unser, Brown, Lunger, etc, all in T332s except Gethin's T430 in seventh place. Redman was sixth after an excursion and an unwarranted tyre stop when it looked as if the rain was stopping; it didn't.

Jackie Oliver made it two non-Lola wins in a row at Elkhart Lake a fortnight later as Redman broke a valve while leading. Unser then had gearbox problems and had to let Oliver through. He finished second. Brian Redman in the T332C returned at Mid-Ohio and outqualified the field by a clear second, dominated the heat and won the final by twenty-nine seconds. Jackie Oliver was second, Danny Ongais in a T332C a luckless third from spinner Unser. Alan Jones did not start the final after experiencing gearbox problems, and so the title race was now wide open again.

Brian then did it again in his Haas/Hall T332C, at Elkhart in late August, with Ongais second and Unser third, both in T332s. Peter Gethin and Teddy Pilette were next up in new T430s. Down to the wire at Riverside, Jones or Oliver needed to win with Redman worse than seventh to deny him his third straight title, but this didn't happen. Al Unser qualified fastest, won his heat and blasted off into the distance. Jackie Oliver (who won his heat) was a distant second in the Shadow Dodge. Redman, who qualified second, cruised home third, just ahead of Jones and Schuppan. Brian had 132 points, Unser (who missed the first two races) had 112, Oliver 108, Jones 96, Ongais 78, Schuppan 45, etc.

Hardly had the dust settled on the season when in mid-November the SCCA announced they were dropping F5000 in lieu of a reformed Can-Am (which had been dormant since end of 1974) with sportscar-bodied F1/F5000 machinery. Carl Haas and Brian Redman were unimpressed and Jim Hall reckoned it wouldn't bring in the punters as hoped ...

Alan Jones in the Theodore T332C won the 1977 Adelaide round of the Aussie 'Tasman' but was out of luck elsewhere as the T400s improved. The same thing happened at the non-championship Calder race a few weeks afterwards, where Max Stewart was killed in a T400. Later, in September, after McCormick had won the first round of the 'Aussie F1' in a McLaren M23 Leyland, A Costanzo, in a T332, won at Sandown from Alan Hamilton in a T430 and Ken Bartlett in a T400.

Holland used an old car to finish fourth in the 1977 Shellsport opener at Snetterton (won by de Villota in a Lyncar DFV) then a new T332C for second at Mallory (won by Guy Edwards in a March V6). Belso in a T330 was third at Snetterton, fourth in Leicestershire. Keith Holland was fifth at Mallory – but Brian McGuire was killed at Brands Hatch the same weekend. Holland split from Gibbs and raced a privateer McRae.

Magee in a T332 was second at Snetterton in Round 13, in October, in a race won by Tony Trimmer in a Surtees TS19, who clinched the title.

Price when new: £5650 (rolling chassis)

9

1973-1977

T33CS – 1977/79 – Can-Am – 12 built

The T333 was taken to an encouraging testing session, with Eric Broadley in attendance, at Rattlesnake Raceway in May 1977. Basically a T332 with wide bodywork, it dominated the early years of the new Can-Am, resurrected (at the expense of F5000) after a two-year hiatus. Things got off to the worst possible start, however, when the pace-setting Redman was seriously injured in practice for the first race in June at St. Jovite. Elliott Forbes Robinson had already flipped his Freeman/Newman T332CS at the notorious 140mph hill (shades of Paul Hawkins and Hugh Dibley in the 1966 Can-Am) without injury when a much faster Redman looped his example – on which he had a long F5000 nose to help keep it down – coming down on the rollover bar from

The T333 Can-Am car of 1977. (Author's collection)

more than twenty feet. The car slid and then flipped back onto its wheels.

Horst Kwech rebuilt Redman's car after the wreck, improving it somewhat over the standard Lola offering, but did not finish the St. Jovite race when the oil cooler detached itself. The race was won by Tom Klausler in a Schkee DB1 which was, in fact, the ex-Gordon Johncock T332 with bodywork and modifications by Doug Schulz and Bob McKee. John Gunn was second and Horst Kroll third, both in Lolas.

At the Laguna Seca Round 2, poleman Klausler in the Schkee did not start (having blown up both its Chevys). Chris Amon in a Wolf Dallara WD1 did not start either due to a vibration, and Haas and Hall were absent – so the series was seemingly going from bad to worse. It got poorer still when Brown in the VDS T332CS broke his ankle and partner Gethin walked out, disillusioned. Don Briedenbach in his T332CS won from Elliot Forbes Robinson, also in a T332CS.

Brian Redman's place in the Haas/Hall team was taken by Patrick Tambay who – despite never having seen Watkins Glen or the car before – won pole at his first attempt and then won the race from flag to flag. That restored morale! Tambay was chased early on by Klauseler in the Schkee and Gilles Villeneuve in a Wolf, but both failed to finish. Gethin was second in the VDS T333CS with Forbes Robinson's version next.

Peter Gethin then won Elkhart Lake, his first victory for four years and at the same track! Patrick Tambay had a huge practice accident but was unhurt,

and the car was rebuilt overnight. David Briggs in a Lola was second and Villeneuve third with Tambay fourth. Schkee had led early on only to hit a backmarker, breaking a wheel. Pole time was six seconds slower than F5000.

Patrick Tambay then won the last five races in the series: Mid-Ohio, Mosport, Trois Rivieres, Sears Point and Riverside. He won from pole at Mid-Ohio but was chased by George Follmer in a Lola until his engine went on lap 37 out of 58. Elliot Forbes Robinson was thus second. Klausler should have been third but got involved with a backmarker again, this time only six laps from the end, and retired. Peter Gethin lost third when his fuel tank ran dry just two laps from home, but he was still classified sixth. Randy Lewis was third and John Gunn fourth, in Lolas.

At the Mosport race, curiously, Tambay's pole time was only a second shy of the F5000 record, and the fastest two-litre was the T296BDX of Bobby Rahal. George Follmer pipped Peter Gethin for second place on the last lap after Forbes Robinson spun out of it and (trying to extricate himself) tapped Peter, giving George the inside line for the last few corners. Elliot Forbes Robinson was fourth. Mike Hall in a T294BDG topped the two-litre class after Rahal's gear linkage went awry.

Trois Rivieres saw Gethin lead initially – until Tambay shuffled past on the tight track. Peter then spun down to third, to Forbes Robinson's benefit. Rahal was sixth in a two-litre Lola.

At Sears Point the Haas/Hall car was followed home by Gethin and John Morton, with Forbes Robinson fourth,

while at Riverside the lead was initially held by Alan Jones in a Shadow until he lost third gear. Tambay passed him and was not headed thereafter. Peter Gethin and Elliot Forbes Robinson both needed repairs so George Follmer was promoted to second. John Morton in a T332CS was third and Gethin finally took fourth. Fifth was the (ex-Gulf) Mirage of Don Pike, and Lola took the top six on points.

Overall length 168ins
Overall width 84ins
Wheelbase 102ins
Front track 64ins
Rear track...................... 64ins

T340/342 – 1973/75 – FF – 213 built

Lola records show that thirty-six T340s were built in 1973 with the bulk of sales following on in the next two years. With a simple spaceframe with easily adjustable suspension to suit individual drivers' needs, the T340 range was a very profitable one for Lola, Formula Ford proving very popular and showing just what Lola was good at producing: an excellent customer car which satisfied all criteria of strength, simplicity and good handling.

In 1973 Frank Gardner was taken to hospital by Eric Broadley for a check-up following a big accident while testing the prototype T340 at Snetterton in June (the cause remains unknown). Regular Snetterton hang-abouter Patrick Neve – quicker than Frank – then constantly matched the lap record while testing the car there.

Works-assisted cars were raced in 1974 Formula Ford by the Shellsport

JNM Team of Robert Joubert (RSA) and Patrick Neve of Belgium, the latter winning the STP title. His 1974 Mallory Park lap record still stood five years later. The team was managed by Peter Mackintosh.

Completion of a T340/342 in May 1975 marked the 1000th Lola.

The T342 of Mike Ford. (Author's collection)

This T342 was the 1000th Lola racing car built. (Author's collection)

T350 – 1975 – F3 – 1 built

On 31 October 1974 *Autosport* announced that Patrick Neve and Robert Joubert were to drive the works T350 F3s in 1975. Lola was back in the formula after many years, their last model being the T362. The new car was based on the T360 Formula Atlantic chassis. (Neve subsequently led the championship in a Safir instead.)

T360 – 1974/75 – FA/FB – 19 built

Richard Scott debuted the T360 at the Silverstone International Trophy of 1974, but it understeered badly. Big improvements were found in post-race testing and the T360 was campaigned on and off thereafter. T360s were seen

in British Formula Atlantic, being campaigned without much success by the likes of Nigel Clarkson, though Scott sometimes used the same car. Indeed Scott got pole position at Thruxton in November. Ted Wentz swapped from a March to a T360 at the same meeting and set the fastest race lap with Scott and also Alan Jones in a March.

Tom Klausler won on the T360's North American debut at Gimli near Winnipeg, and he also won Trois Rivieres from Jean-Pierre Jaussaud in a Chevron B24 and Patrick Depailler in a March. Bill O'Connor was on the front row with Tom Klausler there, but the engine let go. Klausler also led at the United States

Grand Prix support race only for the engine to blow up after thirteen laps out of thirty, bequeathing an easy win to O'Connor. Motor mechanic Klausler was almost FA champion, but the title went to Bill Brack in a modified Lotus 69 called a Crosty.

In 1975 in Britain, Ted Wentz tested a T360B F2 BDG with a conversion from Formula Atlantic specification which took about three weeks to complete at the Team's base, Maurice Gomm's Arch Motors at Old Woking – Broadley and Surtees' old haunt. Wentz wanted to compete in his sponsor Wella's Formula Two at Thruxton and he qualified fifth to Jacques Laffite in a Martini and was third in the first heat to 'Jolly Jacques' and Brian Henton in a March. Wentz was second in the second part when he went onto the grass at Church, trying to avoid a spinning Brambilla, and he holed the radiator. Vittorio recovered to win the race but Laffite took the event on aggregate.

Reverting to Formula Atlantic trim, Wentz was sixth at the Silverstone International Trophy supporter in a race won by Tony Brise in a Modus.

Wentz was second late in the race but then had fuel problems. He was second at Silverstone next month too, again to Tony Brise, and he picked up the same result at Brands Hatch later that May. John Nicholson in a T360B was sixth.

Nick May in a T360B came a surprise second to Brise at Oulton in late May; meanwhile, Wentz's off had dropped him to eleventh despite a stirring comeback. May was then third

to Jim Crawford in a Chevron and Ray Mallock in a March at Mallory Park.

Wentz won the 'big one' from pole position in the British Grand Prix Support at Silverstone. This was a really spirited race with Arlo Lawler driving a Chevron and Brian Muir in a Birrana, Ted winning by 0.4 seconds with the Aussie another 0.1 seconds back after outbraking himself in a last-lap demon attempt to take the lead. He repeated the result a fortnight

A T346 awaits delivery outside the works. (Author's collection)

The T350 F3 Lola at the Racing Car Show of 1972. (Courtesy David Hodges)

later, also at Silverstone, beating Ray Mallock and Richard Morgan in a Wheatcroft. Nick May was second until his car's fuel pump failed after eleven laps. May was again second, at Mallory Park in August, as Crawford, (the winner) closed on Brise (3rd) for the championship. Wentz blew his engine while in the top three.

Ted's Wella car was already in Formula Two trim for the next weekend's meeting at Silverstone, having long-range tanks and deformable structures. He qualified twenty-first out of thirty two. He was fifth after thirty-one out of fifty laps (despite a spin), only to have his Cosworth BDG suddenly cut out on him, losing a probable fourth. Michael Leclere in a March BMW won from Gerard Larrousse in an Elf BMW and super-star Brian Henton in a Wheatcroft BDA.

Gunnar Nilsson won twice at Brands Hatch on consecutive September weekends, first in the wet and then in sunshine. May and Wentz were out of luck in the first encounter, but came in second and fourth respectively the next time around. But it was too little and too late to stop Tony Brise clinching the championship. Yet with the new (Hill) F1 sensation only tenth and then third, the Swede got a psychological edge over the Brit, for sure ...

Gunnar made it five straight wins at the Brands Hatch finale as Wentz did not start due to handling difficulties with the new Lola. Gunnar then saw off Henton, Brise, Riley and all to take an emphatic win. The Formula 3 champion, Gunnar Nilsson, was already testing an F1 car. Final points were Ted 42,

Gunnar 36, Tony 31, Richard Morgan 29, etc.

Nine T360s were entered for the 1975 Canadian series, including Tom Klausler, EFR, Howdy Holmes and Bill O'Connor. March drivers included Gilles Villeneuve and Bertil Roos, who won the Edmonton opener and then Round 2 at Westwood where the pole went to Bobby Rahal in a T360. 'This young newcomer is obviously a guy to watch', said *Autosport*. Joubert went off and team-mate D Walker (also in a T360) had no joy, both having started from the rear. Gilles won a wet Round 3 at Gimli despite starting 19th due to qualifying engine problems. The track inland at Winnipeg was so wet you'd have thought the Atlantic had literally come to town! Rahal was second and Tom Gloy ninth in their respective T360s. EFR won Round 4 at the newly reopened St Jovite (after a four-year absence), and Gilles was second. Klausler in the T360 was third.

Elliot Forbes Robinson won Round 5 too, at Mosport, and Kenny Brack – driving a Chevron B29 – won the final race at Halifax to clinch the third consecutive Canadian Formula Atlantic title. He had led all the way. Dave Walker in a Lola was on the front row but dropped to fourth behind Klausler and Holmes.

Vittorio Brambilla (Austrian GP hero of previous weekend) then won the Trois Rivieres for March, and the locals were humbled by imports – the first championship regulars being Bertil Roos in a March (fifth) and Dave Walker in a Lola (sixth). Next week the status quo was restored when Brack won the

Graham Hill in the Embassy-sponsored T370 at Brands Hatch in 1974. (Courtesy David Hodges)

Donnybrooke non-championship race from poleman Rahal in his T360.

Barry Robinson had the ex-May T360BDG (updated to resemble a T450) in the 1976 European F5000 opener at Mallory Park, but he suffered clutch problems which dropped him back. At Round 2 at Snetterton he was on the back row and didn't feature. He would be eighth at Oulton Park in Round 3 and eighth again at Brands Hatch in June.

Tony Trimmer won the 1976 Indy Atlantic opener at Brands Hatch in a works-loaned Capital Radio T360 from the back of the grid. Missing the opener, Ted Wentz in a T460 was second in the new Swan Lager car to Tony Trimmer in a T360 at Brands Hatch for Round 2 in May. They shared the fastest lap and Trimmer later won at Phoenix Park too.

John Miedecke was sixth in the New Zealand Peter Stuyvesant series 1977 Tasman opener at Bay Park in a T360 and Steve Millen won but thereafter was not a points scorer. Missing out at Pukekohe, John was then fifth at Manfeild, sixth at Teretonga and Christchurch. 5 points equalled 9th in the championship. Rosberg won three out of five races en route to 33 points and Gloy scored one win giving 25 points.

T370 – 1973/74 – F1 (Hill) – 3 built
First tested in secrecy by Gardner at Snetterton in late October 1973, the T370 was for built for Graham Hill's Embassy-backed Formula One team and was the first F1 Lola since the Mark 4 of 1962.

A fortnight later Hill was testing the T370. The team would run two cars in the 1974 Formula One World Championship. They were basically all-white with a wedge nose and an anvil airbox, with twin parallel bottom rear links and radius arms plus a single top link suspension. The prototype was then written off at Silverstone's Copse Corner at the end of November by Graham Hill; no reason was given.

Embassy sponsorship for 1974 was confirmed in January, alongside the Shadow. Guy Edwards was signed to be the second driver. Both had recently tested in the UK and Italy and the team was based at Maurice Gomm's shop and managed by ex-USAC/Shadow man Ray Brimble. The Chief mechanic was Dave Kaylor.

At the Argentine GP for the 1974 season, Hill used T370 chassis number HU1 and qualified seventeenth out of twenty-five, but he was out after 46 laps of 53 with engine problems, when lying tenth. Guy was last on the grid in HU2 and was eleventh after an early pitstop. Switching chassis, Hill was eleventh in Brazil; Edwards was out after only three laps when the engine expired, having started last again. Switching back again for the Race of Champions, neither featured in the results.

Come the South African Grand Prix, there was only HU2 for Hill, who finished twelfth. Then at the Silverstone International Trophy Guy Edwards was back in HU1 (with the unused HU3 in the transporter) but he was unable to better ninth place. Hill crashed out on lap thirty-one at Stowe when something broke at the rear. Edwards failed to qualify HU1 in Spain, and Hill stopped HU2 just after half-distance with a blown engine when lying an unlucky thirteenth in the rain.

Reliability paid off at Monaco when Graham was seventh, Guy eighth. Then, at Sweden, Hill was sixth and Edwards seventh in their best showing to date as the Tyrrell six-wheelers came in first and second. The good run ended at Zandvoort in June, when Hill went out with clutch failure and Edwards retired with fuel system problems, both before half-distance. Graham was thirteenth at Dijon and Guy fifteenth.

Guy Edwards was injured (tangling with Martin Birrane's BT43) during a pre-race Mallory F5000 test, breaking his wrist, and was replaced by Peter Gethin for the British Grand Prix. Peter pipped Graham on the penultimate row of the grid in HU3 but did not start due to the bad driving position. Graham finished thirteenth, six laps behind the winner.

At Nürburgring Guy made a valiant attempt, but pain after only six (long) laps in qualifying meant a non-start, and Rolf Stommelen tried the cockpit for size. Hill was ninth. In the next race Rolf easily outqualified Graham driving HU1 but a puncture on lap fourteen caused a crash. Hill was running at the finish but was unclassified on forty-eight laps out of fifty-four and was ostensibly eleventh. At Monza it was a similar story: Rolf comfortably qualified mid-field with Graham near the back and, while the teamleader finished eighth, the German was out after twenty-four laps when the rear suspension broke. (He had been running eighth before an earlier pitstop.)

Graham Hill took delivery of an Alfa V12 and Stommelen became a sportscar driver for the Italians. Rumours circulated that for 1975 Ray Jessop (ex-Token) would design the cars. Hesketh was thought to be looking at the heavy engine with its high centre of gravity, too.

Stommelen came a superb eleventh at Mosport in qualifying, Graham managing only twentieth. In the race itself Rolf was eleventh and Graham fourteenth, in untroubled runs possibly thwarted by down-on-power engines. Finally, at the United States Grand Prix with Hill still using HU2 and Stommelen again in HU1, Graham had engine problems in practice and Rolf suffered from chassis dramas including a defective hub and electrics. Both were in the last four on the grid with Helmuth Koinnig in a Surtees TS16 and Brambilla driving a March 741. Hill plodded away to eighth, Stommelen twelfth, following a tardy start and two stops with tyre problems. Helmut Koinnig was killed on lap nine, and after the race Denny Hulme announced his retirement. The race winner was Emerson Fittipaldi and he was the champion with fifty-five points. Reggazoni came second with fifty-two and Jody Scheckter third with forty-five. The Hill team's total for year was one point. The *Autosport* annual survey commented that Hill had a reliability record as good as Emmo or Clay – but not their speed!

Bob Evans and Francois Migault both drove Lolas at Goodwood in post-

season testing and the F5000 champion was mentioned as a possible driver if Hill retired.

In 1975 Graham Hill started the season in Argentina with HU2 while Rolf drove HU3. They finished tenth and thirteenth respectively. This was hardly inspiring as Graham awaited the new model. He was twelfth and Rolf fourteenth in Brazil.

The new car was announced in late February. Described as an interim model, type T371, it featured a very different monocoque, lighter, repositioned ancillaries and revised suspension. The T372 was to appear in Spain. There, Rolf qualified the new 371-1 midfield but Graham did not start after crashing on JPS oil in his normal 370-2. The new car was the work of ex-Lola/Shadow penman Andy Smallman (Lola-based in truth) and was constructed at John Thompson's workshop. Rolf finished seventh and unlapped. A good end to a fraught weekend.

Rolf was the sole Hill driver at the Brands Hatch Race of Champions and qualified fifth, finishing ninth to Tom Pryce due to a cracked exhaust affecting his performance.

Graham Hill announced in April that he was to build his own cars, designed – as was the T371 – by Andy

Smallman with the blessing of Eric Broadley. Stommelen's car was now to be called the GH1; Hill's forthcoming attraction the GH2. He appeared first with it at the Silverstone International Trophy, chopping Lella Lombardi's March every time she tried to pass him!

At the next event, the Spanish Grand Prix, Hill stepped aside for Francois Migault, and following a nine-car pile-up at the first corner Rolf found himself third, using GH2. He worked his way into the lead only for a rear wing mount to break on lap twenty-seven, putting GH1 into the crowd, killing four and breaking both the driver's legs. It was the beginning of the end.

Graham Hill used GH1 and T370/3 at Monaco, where he failed to qualify. Stommelen (back from his Spanish injuries) practised it at Monza too and raced a Hill.

Graham Hill (who announced his driving retirement at the British Grand Prix), Tony Brise, Smallman, Brimble and two mechanics were killed at Elstree in November when the aircraft Graham was piloting crashed on the way back from testing a new model at Paul Ricard.

T380 – 1975 – 3-litre Sports – 2 built

A replacement for the T280, the T380, was used in 1975 by Alain de

Cadenet at the Le Mans 24 hours in lieu of the car bearing his own name. It proved to be 15mph slower on the Mulsanne straight. There was nobody from Lola around to help, so the team experimented, finally going back to the original specification. Chris Craft co-drove and Keith Greene team-managed. There were all manner of dramas and delays but Chris was said by the ACO to be credited with the fastest race lap. They finished fifteenth, forty-five laps down, in a race won by Ickx and Bell in a Gulf Ford. Ford Cosworth DFV engines came in first, second and third.

Marco Capoferri was sixth in the 1976 Zolder round of the Interseries in early May and then shared a T390 DFV with Mario Casoni to qualify sixth on the Imola grid for the World Sportscar Championship Round 4. Alas, gearbox problems set in as early as lap three so they did not finish this event but the same pairing did finish tenth at Dijon in Round 6.

The T380 of de Cadenet and Craft came third at the Le Mans 24-hour race, only twelve laps adrift of Ickx and van Lennep in the works Porsche 936 and one lap off the second place Mirage of Lafosse and Migault. This was the best-ever Lola result there, and certainly the best place by a true privateer since Briggs Cunningham's days.

The drivers – sponsored by Tate and Lyle and Hammond's Sauce – qualified tenth in a car now rebodied because of its slow top speed the year before. A shorter tail, repositioned rear wing and lighter bodywork worked. The car was road-registered – and rumour had it that its aerodynamics were tested on the M4! (a British motorway). A terrific 'gentlemen racer' run.

A T390 was pictured in May 1977 in *Autosport*. Not so much a Lola, more a Bitsa, the tub having been built up by John Thompson and with input from Eric Broadley, Len Bailey and Gordon Murray. There were lots of problems, including the loss of fifteen minutes early on with a dragging clutch and then an hour repairing the nose after Chris Craft went off at night in the wet. However, de Cadenet's Tate & Lyle car (with Gordon Spice as reserve driver) finished fifth in that year's Le Mans, only ninety seconds from third place and 230 miles behind the Ickx/Haywood/Barth works Porsche 936 winners.

In the meantime, the de Cadanet/ Lola of 1976 had been sold and was being used by Dorset Racing for Simon Phillips/T.Birchenough/Richard Bond and Brian Joscelyne.

De Cadenet's new chassis was the work of Len Bailey, with suspension by Gordon Murray. Unlike the previous year's car, the engine was a fully stressed member, the DFV putting out 380bhp at 9000rpm. The 'Phillips' car was subsequently tenth at the Hockenheim Interseries in October 1977, driven by Phillips and Bond.

T390 – 1975 – 2-litre Sports – 5 built

Guy Edwards' CI Caravans-sponsored T390, using the Hart two-litre engine, was announced in *Autosport* in April of 1975 and was works-assisted, the Manager being Pat Mackay. Guy gave the model its debut at the Silverstone International Trophy Support race, coming in third behind John Lepp in a March and Ian Grob driving a Chevron. Richard Lloyd was fourth with the Heavens T294. Martin Raymond also had a T390 Hart and finished fifth. The T390 had very advanced rising rate suspension and proved very difficult to set up.

Jorg Obermoser's Warsteiner TOJ BMW won the first round of the European Two-litre Sportscar Championship at Brands Hatch in June. John Hine was first in the opening heat in a Chevron, Edwards second and Obermoser third, but Hine spun and could not restart in the second heat, leaving Jorg to win with Guy again runner-up. The aggregate win went to Obermoser, then Guy Edwards, and then Ian Grob in the Chevron. The Lola apparently handled badly despite Eric Broadley's help. At that point, the new rising rate suspension was still being sorted out.

Jorg Obermoser won the Hockenheim Round 2 on 31 August, the best Lola being Reudi Jauslin – coming in fifth in a T294 – and Guy Edwards, who finished ninth in a T390 with the fastest lap in the second part.

T400 – 1974/75 – F5000 – 15 built

The specification of the T400 series included a single rear wing stay, while mid-mounted small radiators formed a part of the mandatory crushable structure and the area around the footwell was also strengthened. New aerodynamics were in use, the visible differences including a more pointed nose and a 'Ligier teapot' airbox rather than the anvil type. In use (and despite showing tremendous promise in testing) T400s seemed to deteriorate, to the point where drivers said they would rather use T332s for the last two events of the 1975 Tasman series as the new cars didn't handle. Frank Gardner observed, and judged that they did have enormous potential when the rising rate suspension was sorted. Gardner (now an Aussie resident again) said the cars were sophisticated but not complicated.

Meanwhile, on the other side of the pond in the USA, it was a different matter.

T380, bodywork removed, showing the Cosworth DFV engine installation. (Author's collection)

Eric Broadley was out at Rattlesnake Raceway with Brian Redman in early March to resolve overheating and was soon clocking T332-like times after suspension modifications; yet Haas and Hall – like virtually everyone else in USA – reverted to the T332 for the rest of the season. Only a few brave souls like Weitzes tried to tame the

The 2-litre, Group 6 T390, a development of the T290 series, in the factory grounds. (Author's collection)

Scott in the Durex-sponsored T400 in 1975. The McKechnie racing team add support! (Courtesy David Hodges)

T400, yet Redman was forced to use his almost forgotten example at the end of the year in the Riverside finale, after writing-off his T332 in practice. He received a hard-earned third place behind the omnipotent Viceroy pair of Mario Andretti and Al Unser.

The 1975 story in Europe was the emergence of the T400 as the front-running Lola, although Ian Ashley won Round 1 at Brands Hatch and Gordon Spice won Oulton from Guy Edwards, both in T332s, after Pilette had led easily in T400. Three days later, Pilette was fifth at Brands in Round 3, Ashley, in a T400, finished seventh in the first win for David Purley's Chevron GAA.

Scott again, this time at Oulton Park. Note that the snow by the track has not melted completely.
(Courtesy David Hodges)

Thereafter, T400s were somewhat supreme, T330/332s playing second fiddle, though Ashley's T330-2 did win at Thruxton in May to lead the championship into the mid-season break. Evans returned to F5000 from the BRM debacle and won at Snetterton in July in a Sid Taylor T332 from the T400s of Gethin and Scott. Three T332s were next up for Edwards, Ashley and McGuire. Mallory Park and Thruxton went to Pilette in his T400. Alan Jones then won Round 11 on the Brands Hatch club circuit in a RAM March GAA with a new outright record lap. Tony Brise in a Theodore T332 was next and Guy Edwards in the Britannica T332 third, followed by Holland in a T332, Ashley in his T330 and Gethin in a T400.

Thereafter the T400 was too strong for everything else, including the T332, and Teddy Pilette took the title in October.

Warwick Brown in the VDS T430 took the 1977 Australian F5000 series with wins in both the first two events,

159

Data sheet of the T400 F5000 car.

DATA SHEET

LOLA

TYPE T 400

CHASSIS No. HU/400/ Colour

DELIVERED

ENGINE MANUFACTURER	Chevrolet	NUMBER
TYPE/MODIFICATION		
GEARBOX	Hewland DG 300	NUMBER
CROWN WHEEL & PINION RATIO	9:31	GEAR TEETH
CLUTCH	7¼" dia Triple Plate	
STEERING PINION	7 tooth	

	FRONT	REAR
DISCS (Reduce to 10.2")	Lockheed CP2261-88/89	Lockheed CP2261-47/48
CALIPERS	Lockheed CP2271-83/84	Lockheed CP2385-10/11
MASTER CYLINDER	.70 dia	.70 dia
CLUTCH CYLINDER	¾" dia	⅞" dia
SUSPENSION	Unequal Wishbones	Top Link Parallel Lower Links Twin Radius Rods
RIDE HEIGHT	3½" - 3¾"	5¼" - 5½" Under Rear Li[illegible] Crossbeam
CAMBER	½° Neg - ¾° Neg	Nil - ¼° Neg
CASTOR	3° - 3½°	———
TOE-IN	1/16" - ⅛"	1/16" - ⅛"
SHOCK-ABSORBERS (Dry Settings)	Rebound 6-7 Bump 4-5	Rebound 6-7 Bump 4-5
SPRINGS	8B 400	10.5D 250
ROLL BAR	1⅛" dia Alt 1" dia	1" dia Alt ⅞" dia
TRACK	64"	64"
WHEELS	13" dia x 11" Rim	13" dia x 17" Rim
WHEELBASE	102"	
Shock Absorber connecting link centres	13.06"	6.5"

the Australian Grands Prix at Oran Park and Surfers' Paradise. He also gained a second place at Adelaide. VDS team-mate Peter Gethin in a Chevron was runner-up in the first two races, fourth at Adelaide, second in series. Alan Jones was third, winning the final event at Adelaide in a T332C, after lots of dramas in early rounds. Max Stewart finished fourth in the Championship (one win at Sandown), in a T400.

T410 – 1974/76 – FSR – 12 built

Late in November 1974 the new Lola T410 Formula Super Renault made a surprise debut at the Paul Ricard test, beating the new March and a hack Martini (driven by Arnoux and Tambay among others) by a full second when driven by Richard Scott.

Rene Arnoux became the first Formula Super Renault champion with eight wins, and T410s were also driven by Jacques Coulon and Gerard Pilet.

Alain Cudini in a T410 won the Formula Super Renault Round 2 at Nogaro in 1976 – but then Pironi won the next eight races straight! Dallest was third at Magny Cours, Cudini second at Dijon. Alain Prost had his first FSR race at the Dijon round, setting the fastest lap before his engine failed him.

The very next weekend Prost was in a T410 on the second row (alongside Cudini) at the Belgian Grand Prix support race at Zolder, but he slid off on oil when running comfortably with the leading group. After missing out on his ninth straight win – at the French Grand Prix of all places – Didier was back on form at Magny Cours with Alain Cudini second. Pironi was also first at the Italian Grand Prix support race, after Cudini notched pole position only to fall back and then off while holding fourth place. Alain made amends at Nogaro a week later, winning from pole position. Pironi chased hard in the second heat but then had the throttle cable snap. In the penultimate race Cudini outbraked Pironi to win at Ricard, but for the Imola finale Pironi reasserted his authority as Alain had gearbox problems. Nevertheless, Alain Cudini was still runner-up in the championship.

T430 – 1976 – F5000 – 3 built

The T430 was based directly on the T360 Formula Atlantic chassis and was essentially a smaller version of the T300/330/332 series.

The chassis was the same as the T460 (which was then in the throes of replacing the T360) but was wider at the back and with a larger-capacity fuel tank. No panels were common with the Formula Atlantic/Formula Two tubs.

Lola started building the first car immediately after Christmas 1975 and VDS took it to Ricard for evaluation in late February/early March, with a

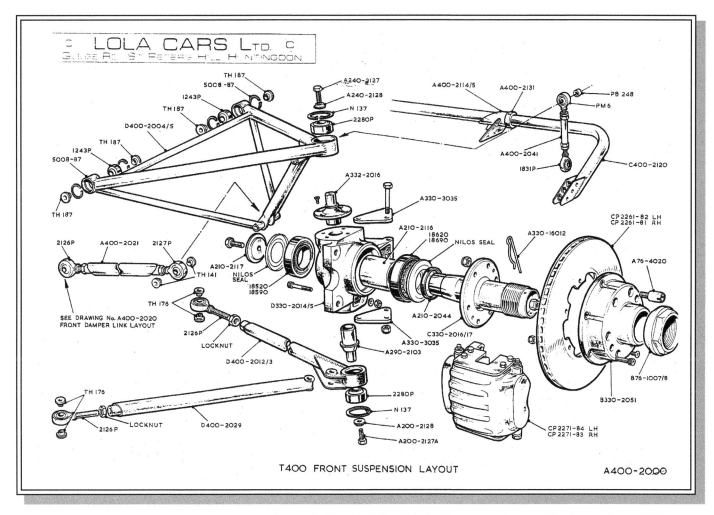

LOLA CARS LTD.
Glebe Rd. St Peters Hill, Huntingdon

T400 FRONT SUSPENSION LAYOUT

A400-2000

new Chevron B37 and an old T400 for a datum baseline, so as to see what to take to USA. The T430 and B37 beat the T400 but were otherwise fairly equal, Lola man Teddy Pilette favouring the T430 while Chevron stalwart Peter Gethin preferred the B37. Chevron did not have enough build capacity, so they took two T430s.

The cars were good, but the Morand prepared engines were not on a par with the Chevrolets of the American engine builders by about 30-50bhp. A deal with Franz Weiss of Chaparral was concluded at the end of the season but it was too little, too late. Hall had a third T430 but he only ran it twice, preferring to stick with the earlier model while it was still winning. VDS T430s were good enough to 'do the business' in Australia afterwards though.

The Lola T450-BMW of Mikko Kozarowitzky outside the works in 1976. (Courtesy David Hodges

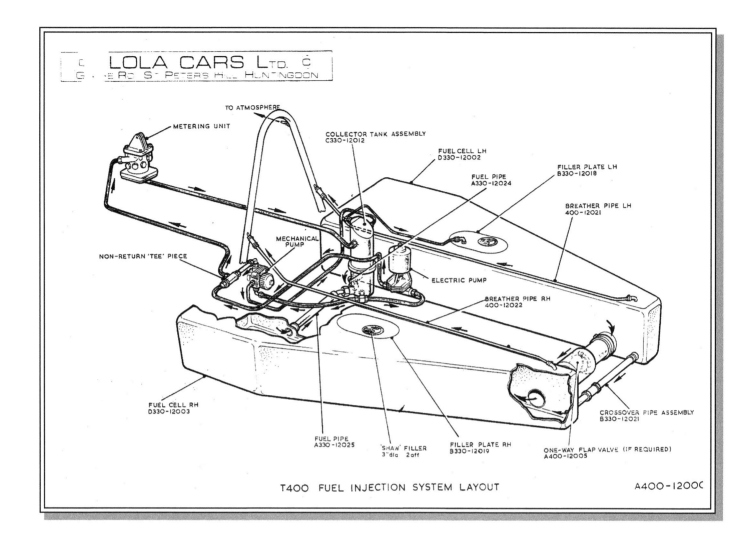

G. … Rd St Peters H.ll Hunt.ngdon

TO ATMOSPHERE

METERING UNIT

COLLECTOR TANK ASSEMBLY
C330-12012

FUEL CELL LH
D330-12002

FUEL PIPE
A330-12024

FILLER PLATE LH
B330-12018

BREATHER PIPE LH
400-12021

MECHANICAL
PUMP

NON-RETURN 'TEE' PIECE

ELECTRIC PUMP

BREATHER PIPE RH
400-12022

FUEL CELL RH
D330-12003

FUEL PIPE
A330-12025

'SHAW' FILLER
3"dia 2 off

FILLER PLATE RH
B330-12019

CROSSOVER PIPE ASSEMBLY
B330-12021

ONE-WAY FLAP VALVE (IF REQUIRED)
A400-12005

T400 FUEL INJECTION SYSTEM LAYOUT

A400-1200C

T440 – 1976/79 – FF – 104 built

Thirty-eight built in 1976.

Chico Serra in a Van Diemen was excluded from his 1977 Oulton Park win in May for passing under the yellow flag, and victory was thus given to Mike Blanchet (who went on to become the Managing Director of Lola) in a T440E. Blanchet was third to Mansell and Serra at Mallory Park in September 1977.

T450 – 1976 – F2 – 4 built

First shown in 1975 and a distinctive looking car. The T450 was tested by 'official unofficial' factory tester Ted Wentz in November; it was a sequel to the disappointing T240 Formula Two of Marko and Gardner back in 1971. The T450 was visibly similar to the ATS Formula Super Vees but with a wide bodywork look. With a Cosworth BDG engine it was under the lap record at Snetterton. Lola Cars were expected to run the 'Philadelphia Flyer' in F2 in 1976 but they didn't. (See T460)

Mikko Kozarowitsky was to race a Lola T450 with a BMW engine in the 1976 F2. Freddy Kottulinsky, a Swedish-domiciled German in his forties, used a Chevron instead. The Wella sponsorship pull-out did not deter Wentz from testing and lapping under the Formula Two record at Silverstone despite cold weather. Ray Mallock, Nick May and Brian Muir all drove a T450 at Snetterton. Ray had done so before at Silverstone, and was impressed.

The T450/60 was revealed on 8 January 1976. A radically new (adjustable) suspension included a narrower track for better grip in low- and medium-speed corners. Ventilated dics with Lockheed four pots calipers were fitted, and the fuel was now all in a central cell to help weight distribution. The F2 had three larger cells than the Formula Atlantic version, totalling twenty-five gallons. New 1977-type Formula Two safety requirements were already built-in regarding rollover, footwell and bulkheads.

Ray Mallock switched to a March for the F2 opener at Hockenheim – the Lola being modified – but problems meant that he did not qualify. Roland Binder qualified his T450 BMW on row ten despite a down-on-power engine while Mikko Kozarowitsky also did not qualify despite having the latest rear suspension modifications.

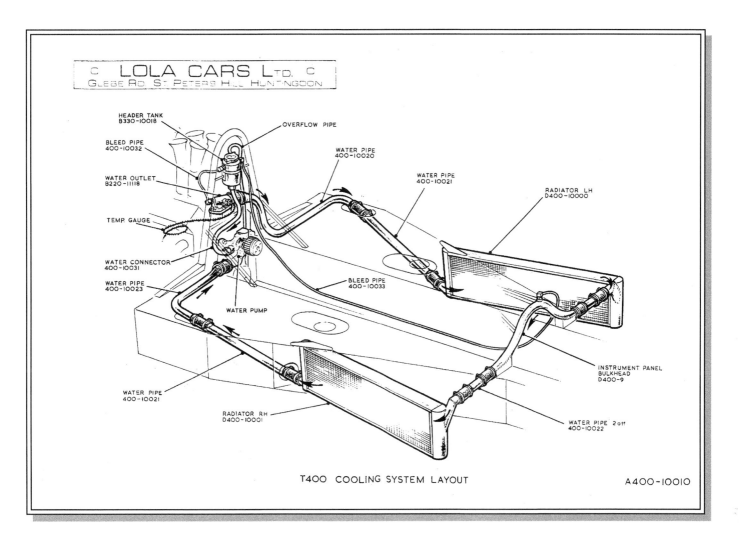

HEADER TANK
B330-10018

OVERFLOW PIPE

BLEED PIPE
400-10032

WATER PIPE
400-10020

WATER PIPE
400-10021

WATER OUTLET
B220-11118

RADIATOR LH
D400-10000

TEMP GAUGE

WATER CONNECTOR
400-10031

BLEED PIPE
400-10033

WATER PIPE
400-10023

WATER PUMP

INSTRUMENT PANEL
BULKHEAD
D400-9

WATER PIPE
400-10021

RADIATOR RH
D400-10001

WATER PIPE 2 off
400-10022

T400 COOLING SYSTEM LAYOUT

A400-10010

For Round 2 at Thruxton, Ian Ashley was in the Ardmore T450BDX instead of Ray Mallock, qualified far back on the grid but nonstarted as he found the car undriveable. Mikko was in at the back of the grid but the car's engine overheated after twenty-one laps. The drivers complained bitterly that the production car was unlike the prototype, with a tendency to spin wheels and break driveshafts with alarming regularity.

Reinhold Joest had his first-ever single-seater race in a modified ATS T410 BMW at Mugello for Round 8. He qualified on the last row and was the first retiree with a blown head gasket after a very few laps. Jabouille in an Elf won from the Martinis of Arnoux and Tambay to keep the championship

lead from the youngsters. There were no T410s at Enna or Estoril. Binder went to the non-championship Misano, qualified last and survived three laps of the first heat (appropriate word!) before his engine boiled over.

New FSV champion Mika Arpiainen qualified his ATS T450 BMW on the penultimate row for the finale at Hockenheim. Sadly, Mika crashed out on lap eight of the first heat, and Jabouille won the race and the championship – by a single point – from Arnoux, third in race. Leclerc, second, held off Rene so as to ensure his team leader won.

T460 – 1976/77 – FAt – 21 built
Following extensive testing by Wentz (and Silverstone lappery by a visiting Bobby Rahal) the 'experimental T360'

made its debut at Oulton Park in October 1975, where Gunnar Nilsson made it three wins from three outings in his Chevron. Wentz was a well-beaten second in the new development Lola, despite a new lap record. It was basically a monocoque with unconventional suspension, whereby although the dampers were placed normally, the coils ran in a direct opposite diagonal to the damper, picking up at the bottom from inside the tub.

Wentz was second to Nilsson at Mallory Park in mid-October, but this was enough to clinch the Southern Organs Championship – Ted had already won the John Player series by a big margin – on the weekend after sponsor bossmen Sidney 'Jim' Miller and John Bellord disappeared ...

*Another shot of a Lola T450.
(Courtesy David Hodges)*

of his three heats. Rouff won at Brands Hatch at the end of the month with Wentz second and Trimmer third.

The following week Ruoff protested against Wentz' tactics as Ted won and Tony ended up in the Druids boonies on the last lap after hectic action on a slippery surface. The protest was upheld. Ruoff won the final round at Oulton in October – as he broke a

The T460. (Author's collection)

The T450/60 was revealed on 8 January 1976. The car shown did not have the bizarre coil arrangement previously referred to. Missing the opener, Wentz in his T460 was second in the new Swan Lager-sponsored car to the older Tony Trimmer T360 at Brands Hatch in May. They shared fastest lap.

Wentz won at Brands in June from Rouff in a Boxer and Scott in a Modus. He also won at Mallory Park in July, from Rouff and Paul Dowsett in a Chevron, and at Knockhill in August he won again from Dowsett and Rouff. Next, at a rebuilt Thruxton, Wentz won two of three heats but a tangle with Rouff in the final left him sixth, the win going to Dowsett. (Ted then used the ex-Kozarowitsky T460 to qualify first in class and sixth overall at the Brands Hatch Shellsport event held over the August Bank Holidays, but he finished only tenth with gearbox problems.) Tony Trimmer in a T460 won at Silverstone in early September after Ted won two

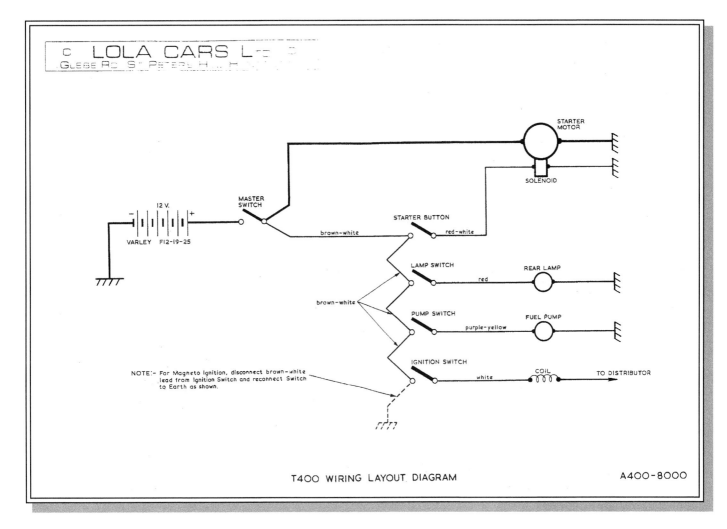

STARTER MOTOR

SOLENOID

12 V.

VARLEY F12-19-25

MASTER SWITCH

STARTER BUTTON

brown-white — red-white

LAMP SWITCH — red — REAR LAMP

brown-white

PUMP SWITCH — purple-yellow — FUEL PUMP

IGNITION SWITCH — white — COIL — TO DISTRIBUTOR

NOTE:- For Magneto Ignition, disconnect brown-white lead from Ignition Switch and reconnect Switch to Earth as shown.

T400 WIRING LAYOUT DIAGRAM   A400-8000

driveshaft – but extra points for gaining pole position ensured him the title. This was subject to the RAC, of course ... which threw out the protest in mid-November.

Bertil Roos finished sixth in the Canadian 1976 Edmonton round where Gilles Villeneuve won in a March. Roos was then third at Westwood in Round 2, won by Marty Loft in a March. Gilles won Gimli/Round 3 from Tom Klausler in his T460 with Wentz ninth (after a spin) in a similar car on his Canadian Formula Atlantic debut one week after the Brands Hatch win. Gilles won St Jovite/Round 4, beating Tom Klausler by ten seconds. Hector Rebaque was eighth in a Haas T460. Gilles won at Halifax/Round 5 from Kenny Brack and took the championship too. Hector Rebaque was fifth. Bobby Rahal in a

March won the last round, Villeneuve being absent. The best Lola was Carl Liebich in a T460 in sixth place. Final points were Gilles 120, Roos 72, Brack 67, Cobb/March 66, Klausler 58, etc.

Early in September Gilles beat Vittorio Brambilla into fourth, James Hunt into third and Alan Jones into second place at Trois Rivieres, winning decisively for March. Klausler, in his T460, started alongside him on the front row but could only manage tenth. Hector Rebaque was the best Lola finisher in eighth place.

Gilles Villeneuve had won three rounds of the 1976 American IMSA series earlier in the year, but when it resumed in late August he had no money to continue, having spent his budget on the Canadian championship. So to Elkhart Lake for Round 4 where,

although Bobby Rahal in a March dominated Mid-Ohio, his engine cut on the last of forty-two laps leaving Klausler in his T460 to win from Price Cobb in a March. It was Klausler's first victory since 1974 and first of the year for Lolas in North America (six in Canada and three in the USA). Gilles was back to win Round 5 at Road Atlanta and then Cobb won the Laguna finale, his first topline victory.

In Europe, Arlo Lawler qualified a brand new T462BDX midfield at Silverstone in the F2 opener but was pushed off the grid with electric problems. He was sixth and eighth in the opening two Shellsport events but suffered a big accident at Oulton Park on Good Friday. He returned to place sixth at Mallory Park in Round 9 in July.

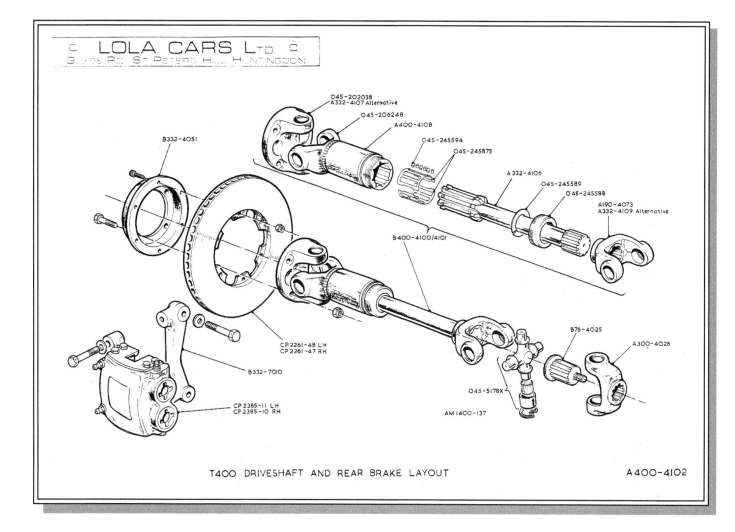

LOLA CARS LTD.
G....RE RD St PETERS HILL HUNTINGDON

B332-4051
045-202038
A332-4107 Alternative
045-206248
A400-4108
045-245594
045-245875
A332-4106
045-245589
045-245588
A190-4073
A332-4109 Alternative
B400-4100/4101
CP 2261-48 LH
CP 2261-47 RH
B332-7010
CP 2385-11 LH
CP 2385-10 RH
B76-4025
A300-4026
045-5178X
AM 1400-137

T400 DRIVESHAFT AND REAR BRAKE LAYOUT

A400-4102

T470 – 1976 – F3 – 1 built
T480 – 1976/77 – SCCA Formula C – 4 built

Based on the T440.

T490/492 – 1976/79 – Sports 2000 – 99 built

Retailing in 1976 at £4,750 plus another £850 for an engine, the Sports 2000 – the new 'Club Class' of motor racing, represented astonishing value for money as the existence of the new 'Sports 2000' series was guaranteed a three-year minimum life-span. The Ford engine was good for 130bhp at 6000rpm, and the new car made its debut at Silverstone Lola Open Day in October. The first one was in Shellsport livery (carrying Race number 13) for Davina Galica. It had been tested by Ted Wentz and John Morrison and

was driven on this auspicious occasion by Derek Bell. It was a three-quarters monocoque with rear subframe, and it was hoped to sell lots of cars in the USA and Italy. The bulk of the suspension was as the single-seater Formula Ford Lola 2000 but uprights were new, made of steel for the fronts and Magnesium alloy at the rear. A brake balance bar was incorporated. Ostensibly the T490 was a cutdown T294.

Brands Hatch used a T490 as racing school trainer. The first year of the new Sports 2000 category started at Oulton on Good Friday 1977, and the series was won by modsporter John Cooper from Davina Galica, both in T490s. Third was John Webb in a Tiga. Lola won nineteen of the twenty rounds. *(See Appendix)*

T496/497 – 1977/79 – SCCA C Sports – 10 built

The T496 used 8 inch front and 10 inch rear width wheels and would use a 1300cc motor. It was basically a T490/492 with F3 gearbox and wheels for American sports car racing or hillclimbs, plus a rear wing and lights. Guiseppe Castellano took the 1977 SCCA 'Run Offs' with a T497 with Lola taking the class for the next three years too.

T500 – 1977/79 – Indy – 5 built

The T500 marked a winning return for

Opposite, top: The very successful sports 2000 T490 prototype at the factory's premises. (Author's collection)

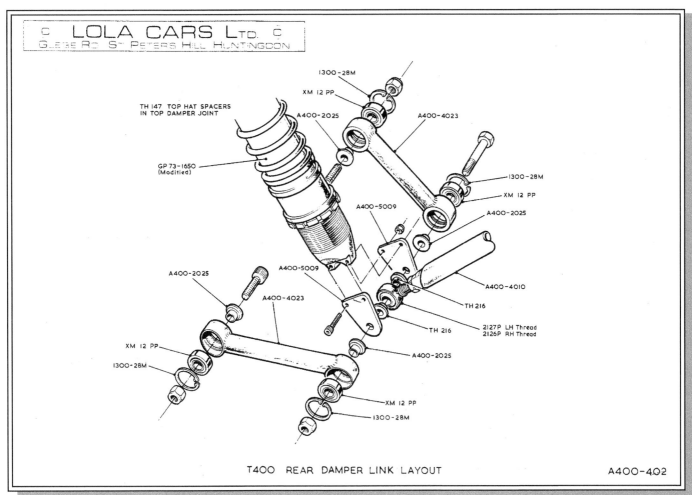

LOLA CARS LTD.
GLEBE RD ST PETERS HILL HUNTINGDON

TH 147 TOP HAT SPACERS
IN TOP DAMPER JOINT

1300-28M

XM 12 PP

A400-2025

A400-4023

GP 73-1650
(Modified)

1300-28M

XM 12 PP

A400-5009

A400-2025

A400-4010

A400-2025

A400-5009

TH 216

A400-4023

TH 216

2127P LH Thread
2126P RH Thread

XM 12 PP

A400-2025

1300-28M

XM 12 PP

1300-28M

T400 REAR DAMPER LINK LAYOUT

A400-402

167

Lola to USAC racing. And how! Rumours of Al Unser having signed with Haas/Hall and a Lola USAC car were confirmed at the end of October 1977. Hugh Absalom was chief mechanic along with Dennis Swan, with the chassis being looked after by Troy Rogers. The engines were built by Franz Weiss.

The car itself was narrow and long with the largest wheelbase ever seen at Indianapolis at 110 inches. The dimensions were as follows:

Overall length 79in
Overall width 44in
Wheelbase 110in
Front track 57in

Rear track 61in

The T500 debuted at Phoenix for Round 1 in the Jimmy Bryan 150 on 18 March, but ran out of fuel thirteen laps from the finish when fifth. Gordon Johncock in a Wildcat won from team-mate Steve Krisiloff and A J Foyt driving a Coyote.

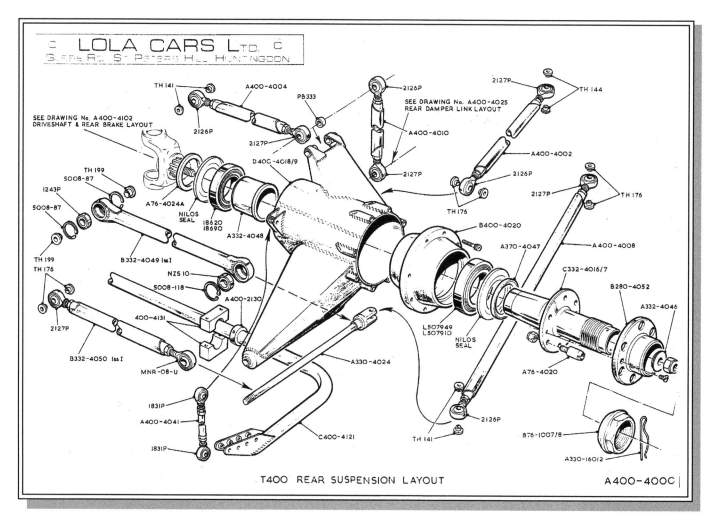

T400 REAR SUSPENSION LAYOUT   A400-4000

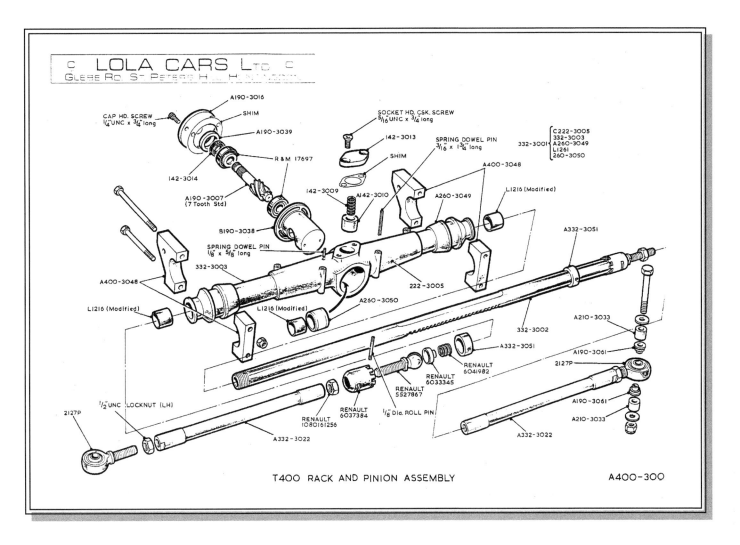

© LOLA CARS Ltd ©
Glebe Rd. St. Peters H. Huntingdon

T400 RACK AND PINION ASSEMBLY   A400-300

At Ontario, Round 2, Unser was third behind Danny Ongais driving a Parnelli and Tom Sneva in a Penske. The car was then destroyed in practice for the Texas 200 at College Station for Round 3, a broken halfshaft being suspected. Al suffered amnesia for four days.

Missing the Trenton Round 4, an untested new car was built for the Indianapolis 500, but the driver and car were unable to approach Unser's pre-crash testing speeds. They still started fifth, and after battling awhile took the winning lead on lap 145, when Danny Ongais blew his engine. Sneva was second (as the previous year), eight seconds in arrears, with Gordon Johncock third. It was the first Indy 500 win for the Ford Cosworth DFX. (Unser

had also won there in 1971/1972, both times in an Offy-powered Johnny Lightning Special, an undisguised Lola copy built by George Bignotti).

Danny Ongais won the Mosport Round 6 on (the then) only USAC road course in North America, but Al crashed out of third place after hitting the guard rail and the car was destroyed.

Another new car was then built for Milwaukee and Round 7, but from the lead Al ran dry of fuel – after 144 out of 150 laps – and dropped to sixth place. Milwaukee saw the maiden USAC win for Rick Mears in a Penske, who also ran out of fuel as he crossed the line.

The Pocono 500, Round 8, saw Al Unser start tenth and finish 24 seconds clear of Johnny Rutherford in a McLaren and Sneva in a Penske. Unser had

nine stops to their twelve and fourteen respectively. He paced himself so as not to use up tyres, and did not need to make any rubber stops at all, only fuel. Rick Mears missed the race as Mario Andretti was back from Formula One for a while. He did not finish.

On to Michigan, where Al had an engine let go. At Atlanta for Round 10 it was like Milwaukee all over again: Unser ran out of fuel and Mears won. Returning to College Station, the battle was between the two Texans with Foyt in a Coyote getting it over Rutherford. Steve Krisiloff was third but was flattened by Foyt in the post-race press conference for suggesting that A J had passed him under a yellow flag.

Ongais won at Milwaukee for Round 12, Unser only managing

Mike Ostroumoff drives his Bordesley Garage-entered T490, a car he used to follow on to his Lola Mark 1. Mike later went on to share a Porsche 908 with Dickie Attwood in historic racing, and after that ran a T70 Mark 3b coupé and a T222 for John Hunt. (Courtesy David Hodges)

fifth place. Ontario saw Foyt out in a Parnelli, the only man to go over 200mph, but he stayed in mid-field as he qualified on the second day. Sneva thus got pole but crashed out early on. Foyt retired on the first lap with gear selection problems, so Johnny Rutherford led until his engine blew. Gordon Johncock then led until his fuel tank ran dry five laps from home. Big Al Unser wins again! Second was Pancho Carter after a big spin, five laps down, and only five cars made the finish. Al, who had started on third row, now led the championship from Sneva and Johncock.

Danny Ongais won the return encounter at Michigan in September, coming from the back row in his Interscope Parnelli. Unser, alas, wrote off his third chassis of the year

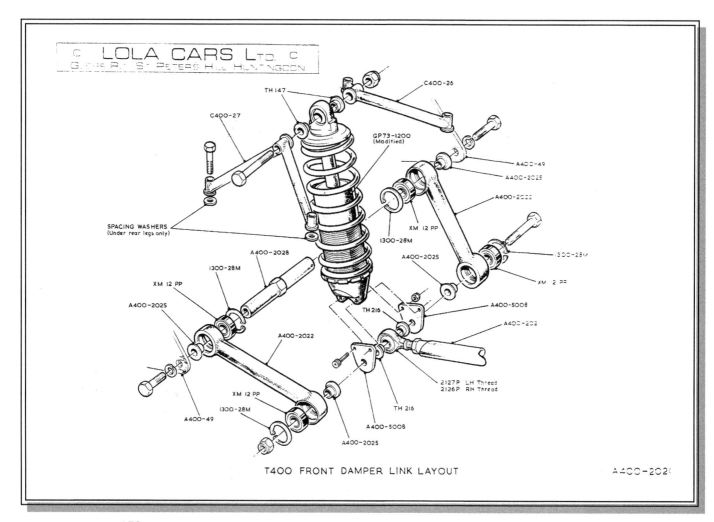

T400 FRONT DAMPER LINK LAYOUT

when trying to squeeze between Spike Gehlhausen and the wall after the Eagle's Offy blew an engine and spun on its own oil, leaving Al nowhere to go.

Mario Andretti had just won the World Championship and celebrated with victory at Trenton, his first USAC win in five years. Foyt was on pole with the Parnelli. Near the end, as the championship contenders Unser and Sneva battled, both tried overtaking second-placed Johnny Parsons in a Lightning Offy, touching wheels. Chastened, Parsons stayed ahead but Tom beat the Lola to the line. (Phew!)

The team was working hard to overcome instability problems, changing suspension geometry and moving pick-up points, etc. They made the car better but not good, Al declaring 'there is a design fault'.

A J Foyt won at Silverstone in what he admitted to be an outdated and overweight old Coyote, the race culminating with only thirty-eight of its scheduled fifty-two laps run, due to rain. Danny Ongais had been on pole again, with Unser second.

Obviously Al's F5000 road racing experience was put to good advantage. Unfortunately he broke a crownwheel and pinion after only twenty-six laps, being classified tenth, with championship rival Sneva third behind Mears, both in Penskes.

Rick promptly went one better at Brands Hatch one week later – but only when Ongais' clutch broke. The Hawaiian had led all eighty-three out of one hundred laps and had a full one-lap advantage on the field. Al did not even get that far: his clutch

exploded as the team took the flag on the rolling start. Sneva avoided an errant spinner early on to claim second in a Penske 1-2.

For the final at Phoenix Ongais again dominated the field, but fell foul of a new pitlane safety ruling which made him lose time, eventually to finish fourth. Johnny Rutherford won from Foyt and Johncock. Al Unser was fifth, not good enough to take the title despite Sneva being only sixteenth having lost seventeen laps with a broken turbo.

Tom Sneva was thus the first-ever USAC champion without a win. Sneva 4153 points, Unser 4031, Johncock 3548, Rutherford 3067, Foyt 3024, etc.

T506/506B – 1977/81 – Mini Grand Prix – 109+ built
T510 – 1977 – FSR – 4 built

Jean-Louis Bouquet's 1977 run of three Formula Super Renault victories was stopped when he was beaten into second place at Rouen for Round 4 by Alain Prost in a Martini. By September Prost led the championship, a position he would not relinquish.

T550 – 1976-1977 – F2 – 1 built

Note – F2 sometimes referred to as T550, by others as T560

Engined by the Holbay Abarth inline six Type 260 designed by the Ferrari designer Iacoponi: the engine resembled one bank of a Ferrari F1 V12. Three engines were tested by Holbay with six more to follow. A production run of twenty-five was expected and 320bhp at 11200rpm was claimed.

Unfortunately it only ever saw

action in anger once all season, Brian Henton in a Wheatcroft doing a single practice session for the 1976 Thruxton Formula Two event before problems occurred, the engine running its bearings. The entry was scratched.

At their Open Day at Silverstone early in October, Derek Ongaro said that Lola were no longer interested in building cars for Formula Three or Two. (After the T450 debacle this was no surprise.)

In February 1977 Ted Wentz in February was testing a new Lola Abarth F2 car at Snetterton. He was returning to the USA soon so probably the car was to be raced by Roberto Marazzi, a twenty-five-year-old Roman who had previously put in some respectable outings in a Trivellato Chevron.

Marazzi tried to qualify the Lola T560 Holbay Abarth for the 1977 F2 opener at Silverstone but failed after blowing up *both* his engines in practice.

In December, both Bob Evans and Bruce Allison had recently tested the 'T560', now with a much more reliable and glorious-sounding Abarth engine. Rumour had it that the car was recently shunted, so now it needed working on too!

T570 – 1977 – F3 – 4 built

Ian Ashley tried qualifying the just-finished T570 for the 1977 Silverstone F3 season opener in March, but it was too slow. Brake problems meant unbalanced cornering, and so on. The car was withdrawn until more test miles had been covered and the bugs sorted out.

The T570 Nova Toyota of George Aposkitis at Brands Hatch. (Author's collection)

Nigel Mansell raced his first 'real' F3 in a T570 at Silverstone in October, having previously only had seat-time in a fraught Puma. He came in fourth, the best result for the marque in European Formula Three all year. At one point he had been up to second! Six weeks later Mansell was fifth at Thruxton, confirming his promise. The *Autosport* seasonal review said: 'Lola ran their T570 model all year but with little hope until they recruited the services of the brilliant young Nigel Mansell who gave the Huntingdon firm much better prospects for the future.'

Nigel Mansell's T570 F3 car outside the factory. It was this car that really started Nigel on his way to the top in motor racing and in which he had many fine drives. (Author's collection)

Tony Steele in his Mark 2 Lola. (Courtesy Dave Cundy)

Bob Evans 'all crossed up' in the Alan McKechnie-owned T332 in a Formula 5000 race. (Courtesy David Hodges)

SL76/148, the
ex-Pico Troberg
1969 T70
Mark 3B coupé
being raced, in
later years, by
Jonathan Baker.
(Courtesy
Dave Cundy)

A 1959 Lola Mark 1 taking part in the Sytner CC Cars race at Brands Hatch in 1989. (Courtesy Dave Cundy)

Tony Steele's Mark 2 dicing with an Elva at Brands Hatch. (Courtesy Dave Cundy)

A Thundersports race in 1989 at Brands Hatch. Gregg Hart leads the pack in his T212, a car with which he had great success. (Courtesy Dave Cundy)

Below left: Brands Hatch, 1989, and David Pratley races his Mark 2, a car he has campaigned for many years. (Courtesy Dave Cundy)

Tony Steele in his Mark 2 after overtaking a Cooper Bristol at Brands Hatch in 1990. (Courtesy Dave Cundy)

Brands Hatch, 1984. Nick May in his T70 Spider. (Courtesy Dave Cundy)

David Piper takes part in an historic race in SL76/148, his T70 Mark 3B coupé of 1969, at Brands Hatch in 1989. (Courtesy Dave Cundy)

APPENDIX
SPECIFICATIONS

Mk 2 (see page 12)

Chassis	Tubular spaceframe.
Engine	Ford 105E, tuned by various concerns; 997cc, 4 cylinders. 2 x Weber 40DCOE2 carburettors.
Wheels	Magnesium bolt-on.
Steering	Lola rack and pinion.
Brakes	Lockheed 9in diameter with Alfin drums, inboard at rear.
Suspension:	
Front	Transverse wishbones and coil spring/damper units.
Rear	Unequal length transverse wishbones and coil spring/damper units.
Transmission:	
Clutch	7.25in dry plate.
Gearbox	Modified BMC 'A' Series, 4-speed plus reverse.
Dimensions	Overall length: 10ft 8in; width: 4ft 4in; height 3ft.
Wheelbase	6ft 10in; track: (front) 3ft 9in; (rear): 3ft 9.25in.
Ground clearance	4.25in.

Mk 3 (see page17)

Chassis	Tubular spaceframe.
Engine	Ford 105E tuned by Superspeed – 997 and 1096cc, 2 x Weber 40DCOE2 carburettors.
Wheels	Magnesium bolt-on.
Steering	Lola rack and pinion.
Brakes	Lockheed 9in diameter with Alfin drums, Inboard at the rear.
Suspension:	
Front	Transverse wishbones and coil spring/damper units.
Rear	Unequal length transverse wishbones and coil spring/damper units.
Transmission:	
Clutch	7.25in single dry plate.
Gearbox	Modified Volkswagen all-syncromesh.
Dimensions	Overall length: 12ft; width: 4ft 7in; height: 2ft 10in.
Wheelbase	7ft 4in; track: (front) 4ft 1in; (rear) 4ft.
Ground clearance	3.5in.

Mk 5/5A (see page25)

Chassis	Tubular steel spaceframe.
Engine	Ford 105E-1097cc Cosworth or Holbay tuned.
Wheels	3in magnesium alloy.
Steering	Rack and pinion.
Brakes	9.25in Girling disc brakes.
Suspension	Coil spring/damper units all round, inboard at front; outboard at rear. Paired radius rods all round.
Front	Top wishbone.
Rear	Lower wishbone.
Transmission:	
Clutch	Diaphragm spring.
Gearbox	Hewland Mark 4.
Overall length	144in.
Wheelbase	92in; track (front) 48in; (rear) 48in.

T300 (see page 125)

Chassis	Aluminium alloy monocoque, using engine as a semi-braced member.
Engine	Chevrolet V-8, 305in³. (5000cc).
Gearbox	Hewland DG300, 5-speed plus reverse, LSD fitted.
Suspension:	
Front	Double wishbone, outboard dampers/coil springs plus adjustable anti-roll bar.
Rear	Wide based bottom links with diagonal bracing, fully adjustable; Transverse top links with radius arms, anti-roll bar and outboard coil spring/damper units.
Brakes	Girling 10.5in diameter ventilated discs, outboard at front, inboard at rear.
Steering	Rack and pinion.
Fuel tanks	Safety rubberised fabric cells in monocoque: capacity 30 US gallons.
Wheels	Split rim, cast magnesium, 11in wide at front, 16in at rear.
Dimensions	Wheelbase 101in; front track 58in; rear track 58in; overall length 138in; height (to top of rollbar) 35in; weight 1360lb.

T490/492 (see page 166)

Engine	Titan-modified Ford 1993cc.
Bore	90.8mm.
Stroke	76.9mm.
Power	128-130bhp at 6000rpm.
Lubrication	Dry sump.
Transmission	Hewland Mark 9 Transaxle, 4-speed plus reverse, alloy driveshafts with CV joints.
Chassis	Monocoque with rear tubular space frame. Riveted and bonded by bronze and argon welding. Colour impregnated GRP nose and tail sections.
Suspension	Fully adjustable, double wishbone at front, lower wishbone and upper link with radius rods at rear. Rack and pinion steering.
Brakes, wheels & tyres	Disc brakes all round, 9.5in by 0.275in solid discs, Lockheed calipers, inboard mounted at rear. 13in diameter wheels by 6in width.

Also from Veloce Publishing –

Reprinted after a long absence! The definitive development and racing history of the Lola T70. John Starkey has compiled a huge amount of information on the cars and interviewed many past and present owners and drivers about their experiences with the T70. Contains the history and specification – where known – of each individual T70 chassis.

ISBN: 978-1-787110-51-9
Paperback • 25x20.7cm • 192 pages • 220 pictures

For more info on Veloce titles, visit our website at www.veloce.co.uk
• email: info@veloce.co.uk • Tel: +44(0)1305 260068

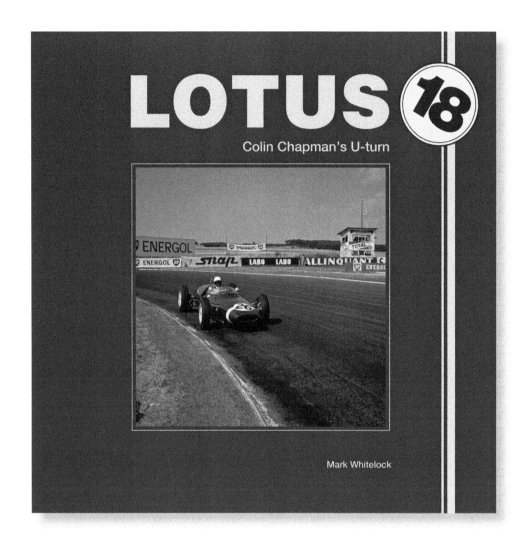

LOTUS 18

Colin Chapman's U-turn

Mark Whitelock

In 1960, Colin Chapman sought to identify the most straightforward and uncomplicated way of building a Formula 1 car. The result was his first rear-engined design, the trendsetting Lotus 18. This book charts the 18's competition history, from its inception, up to 1966 – via sensational victories over Ferrari at Monaco and the Nürburgring.

ISBN: 978-1-845845-20-9
Hardback • 24.8x24.8cm • 192 pages • 159 colour and b&w pictures

For more info on Veloce titles, visit our website at www.veloce.co.uk
• email: info@veloce.co.uk • Tel: +44(0)1305 260068

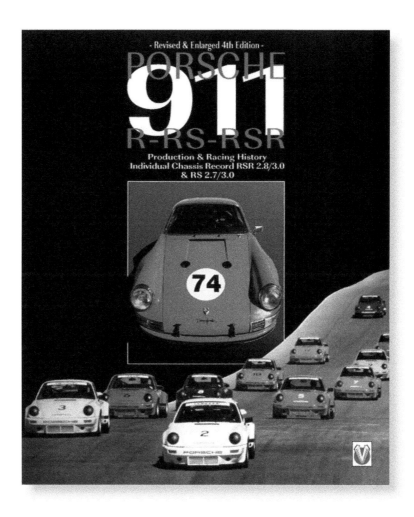

The long-established, definitive history from inception to racing record, now
in its 4th edition. Completely revised and updated, and increased from 192
to 272 pages. Now has an individual chassis database for 1584 1973 RS
2.7 models. Revised and enlarged edition of what has become the standard
reference work on the Rennsport 911s.

ISBN: 978-1-845847-22-7
eBook • flowing text • 200 pictures

For more info on Veloce titles, visit our website at www.veloce.co.uk
• email: info@veloce.co.uk • Tel: +44(0)1305 260068

INDEX